Men-at-Arms • 16

Frederick the Great's Army

Albert Seaton • Illustrated by Michael Youens

Series editor Martin Windrow

First published in Great Britain in 1973 by Osprey Publishing,
Midland House, West Way, Botley, Oxford OX2 0PH, UK
44-02 23rd St, Suite 219, Long Island City, NY 11101, USA
Email: info@ospreypublishing.com

Transferred to digital print on demand 2010

First published 1973
2nd impression 2002

Printed and bound by PrintOnDemand-Worldwide.com, Peterborough, UK

A CIP catalogue record for this book is available from the British Library

ISBN: 978 0 85045 151 1

Series Editor: Martin Windrow
Index by Fineline Editorial Services

Acknowledgements
In the preparation of the plates, illustrations and text, acknowledgement is made to
Accurate Vorstellung der sämtlichen Koniglich Preussischen Armee by von S. I. C. H.
(1759) Lange's *Die Soldaten Friedrichs des Gross en* (1853) and Knötel's *Uniformkunde*
(1890–1909); and to Macaulay's *Frederick the Great* and Carlyle's *Life of Frederick
the Great*. The photographs are produced by courtesy of the Keeper, the Library
of the Victoria and Albert Museum (photographer Berkhamsted Photographic,
Berkhamsted, Hertfordshire).

The Woodland Trust
Osprey Publishing is supporting the Woodland Trust, the UK's leading woodland
conservation charity, by funding the dedication of trees.

www.ospreypublishing.com

The Rise of Prussia and Hohenzollern

The history of Prussia had its origin in Brandenburg, the wood- and lake-studded sandy wastes between the middle Elbe and the lower Vistula. The country had been occupied by Slavonic Wends before being settled by Germans, and from 1320 onwards it was ruled by the Bavarian Electors and then by the Princes of Luxembourg before reverting to Sigismund, the Holy Roman Emperor. Sigismund was in debt to Frederick Hohenzollern, the Burggrave of Nuremberg, for 150,000 gulden, and had mortgaged the Electorate of Brandenburg as security for the loan; and, since the Emperor saw no possibility of repaying the sum, he agreed in 1415 that on payment of a further 250,000 gulden, Brandenburg, with its land and titles, together with its sovereign electorship, should pass to the Hohenzollerns for ever. Sigismund thought himself well rid of it, for Brandenburg was a poor province; even around Berlin, its new capital, the country was almost a desert, the sandy soil yielding the thinnest crops of rye and oats only in places; and where there was not open heath there was primeval forest and swamp.

Farther to the east, in the territory lying between the Vistula and the Memel, against the Baltic shore, lived the Prussians, a warlike and heathen people, ethnologically related to the Lithuanians and Latvians but entirely distinct from both Teuton and Slav. The Prussians had for some time successfully resisted the encroachments of the Christian German and the Pole, but they were eventually overcome by the crusading Order of the Teutonic Knights. The country was then resettled by German colonizers, the original Prussian inhabitants having been killed, driven out or assimilated by the conquerors; by 1400 the land between Pomerania and Lithuania continued to be known as Prussia and then, by association, the name was applied to the new German inhabitants.

The Knights of the Teutonic Order, by the sanction of the Pope and the German Emperor (although Prussia in fact lay outside the territories of the Holy Roman Empire) continued to rule the new colony. In 1410 the Order was defeated in battle at Tannenberg by Jagellon of Poland, and in 1466 it was forced to cede West Prussia, retaining East Prussia only by admitting allegiance to the Polish king. The Order, corrupt and failing, chose a Hohenzollern to be its Grand Master, but he, becoming a Protestant, in 1525 followed the

A soldier of 1 Dragoons and a trumpeter of 12 Cuirassier Regiment

advice of Luther and secularized the religious order, converting its property, virtually the whole of East Prussia, into a private estate for himself and his successors. In 1569 the Hohenzollerns of the two family branches of Brandenburg and of East Prussia entered into a contract whereby, in the event of one or other line dying out, the territories of both branches should be joined under a single ruler. In 1618, on the death of Duke Albert of Prussia, East Prussia was finally joined to the Electorate of Brandenburg. Although East Prussia remained subject to the Polish crown, its accession more than doubled Brandenburg territory, and, since East Prussia was much richer than the original Hohenzollern Mark, it brought with it a great increase in wealth.

During the Thirty Years War (1618–48) Brandenburg was laid waste by imperialist and Swede, Protestant and Roman Catholic; the weak Elector deserted Berlin to find refuge in his East Prussian capital at Königsberg, where he died in 1640. Brandenburg's recovery and its emergence as Prussia, a European power, really dates from the rule of his successor George William, later known as the Great Elector, the great-grandfather of Frederick the Great.

When the Great Elector came to power his exchequer was empty and his country was in ruins, for in no part of the empire had the war been so disastrous as in Brandenburg. Berlin had only 300 citizens left and the population of the whole state numbered less than a million. The Great Elector restored law and order with an iron hand, for he was an unrelenting autocrat, and the absolute power he wielded over his subjects was that of life and death. Tolerant only in matters of religion, and doing away with any remaining municipal freedoms, he laid the foundations for the Hohenzollern Prussian State with its many contradictions and anomalies; its veneration of the civic virtues of industry, honesty and duty so curiously linked with the barbarity and brutality of its rulers and servants of state, which were to make Prussia so hated and feared throughout Germany.

In 1640, however, the Great Elector was unknown and Prussia was little regarded. Its ruler was a supplicant to the kings of Poland, Sweden and England; he bought off the Swedes and began the gigantic task of restoring his Electorate, by energy, thrift and good management. At the Peace of Westphalia he was granted the rich territories of Magdeburg, Halberstadt and Minden in West Germany. He attracted immigrants from West Germany and Holland and used Dutchmen's skills to reclaim the swamps. He helped Sweden against Poland and Poland against Sweden, obtaining Poland's formal relinquishing of its feudal rights over Prussia. And he acquired Cleves, Mark and Ravensberg for Brandenburg. Eventually, before the close of his rule, he became outstanding as a soldier, raising an army of 27,000 trained and well-equipped troops. In 1675, at Fehrbellin near Berlin, acting against the advice of his generals, he attacked and routed a numerically superior force of Swedes. The qualities of the Great Elector were much admired by his great-grandson Frederick the Great for, by the time of his death in 1688, he had raised Brandenburg-Prussia to the rank of one of the first military powers in Northern Europe, leaving to his son, as Macaulay said, 'a principality as considerable as any which was not called a kingdom'.

Prussia the Kingdom

The Great Elector's son Frederick (1688–1713) was a ruler of a different stamp, for he was obsessed with the pursuit of culture, pomp, ostentatious pageants and the outward trappings of majesty. After William of Orange became King of England, Frederick urged upon the Habsburg Emperor that he, too, should be permitted to become a king, not of course of Brandenburg, an electorate within the empire, but of Prussia (strictly speaking East Prussia) which stood outside the imperial frontiers. The Emperor agreed; for Frederick had always taken care to maintain friendly relations with Vienna, and the Emperor could hardly have regarded Brandenburg-Prussia as a rival to Austria's hegemony in Germany.

In 1701 the Elector was crowned King of Prussia in Königsberg, and to mark the occasion he inaugurated the Order of the Black Eagle, a prize of service to the state. Thereafter, by degrees, the title and designation of Prussia began to be applied to Brandenburg and the other scattered German territories over which the Elector ruled from his Brandenburg capital of Berlin. The new king, except for his frivolous obsessions, was very sane, and, although quick-tempered, was affable. He had done some soldiering in his youth, but he was not a man of war. Yet even he regarded a large Prussian Army as being essential to the state; not only for the defence of the realm but also for the maintenance of his own dignity and station. Whereas he had inherited 27,000 men from his father, in time he increased this strength to 50,000. Some of these troops saw active service under the Austrian Prince Eugene, and many of Frederick the Great's latter-day generals received their baptism of fire at Blenheim, Hochstädt, Cassano, Turin and Malplaquet.

Frederick William, who came to the throne in 1713 as the second King of Prussia, took his name from the Great Elector. His outlook and qualities were again different from those of his father, for he had served under Marlborough and he was obsessed with military matters, not so much with campaigning as with the raising and training of soldiers; drill and the minutiae of uniform were among the chief interests of his life. His mind was ill-regulated and he certainly lacked a sense of proportion. From his father he inherited a love of military pomp and ceremonial. He wasted a small fortune in recruiting from abroad a regiment of giants, whereas any stout youth of five feet eight would, in all probability, have made a much more valuable soldier. Yet his army of 60,000 troops were disciplined and drilled to such a standard that would have shamed the household regiments of Versailles and St. James.

Frederick William had many sterling qualities, among them a talent for administration; and he regarded industry and frugality as the highest virtues. On the day after the late king's funeral he discharged every court official, cut the pension list to one-fourth and reduced the thousand saddle-horses in the royal stables to thirty. By this means he brought down household and adminis-

A musketeer and officer of 22 Infantry Regiment. Formed in 1713 it saw no action until 1744 at Prague

trative expenses to one-fifth of the previous cost. He regarded himself as the foremost soldier and the first servant of the realm, working and living under the eye of an imaginary master, Prussia. He was in his office at day-break and expected his ministers to do the same. At midday his ministers and staff dined with him on soup or boiled beef and each was charged for his meal. While he kept himself and his household in squalid poverty, each day called for endless toil as he struggled to check every detail of government, steadily amassing treasure and the finest standing army of the time.

By nature Frederick William was a bully, at times so violent and irrational as to give rise to doubts as to his sanity. For him the sceptre was but a cudgel, for he beat his children and his ministers and flung his judges down the stairs. He prided himself on being German to the bone and spent his nights in the Tobacco Parliament with his drinking and smoking cronies, among them the Pomeranian counsellor Grumbkow, and his Commander-in-Chief Leopold of Anhalt-Dessau, 'the Old Dessauer'. He loathed the French, hated the English and had a contempt for higher education.

5

The sergeant-king's royal power was absolute and, by careful administration, the Prussian population of two and a half million was obliged and able to support a peace-time army of eighty-three thousand.

The Crown Prince Frederick

The future Frederick the Great was born in 1712, the son of Sophia of Hanover and grandson of George I of England. Two older sons had died in infancy and Frederick himself appears to have been an ailing and sickly child. Because his governess was a French Huguenot, French became his mother tongue, for he spoke and wrote German indifferently; he knew no Latin or English. At seven years of age his schooling passed into the hands of a French tutor and two officers, and his education was henceforth based on military subjects, a study of contemporary history (and in particular the history of Brandenburg), economy and administration. At the age of nine he became the commander of a company of a hundred cadets.

Frederick soon came to hate his life at Wusterhausen, his father's residence outside Berlin; he had no liking for hunting or for the buffoonery of the Tobacco Parliament. To his father's disgust, he acquired a taste for French literature and culture, and spent his leisure in learning to play the flute. The father began to hate the son, whom he regarded as effeminate, and the king considered making Frederick's younger brother crown prince in his place. Horrified at his son's delight in soft living and dissipation and at his distaste for the army, he became convinced that he had fathered a monster, a traitor to the Hohenzollerns, who, when he became king, would ruin Prussia. He insulted and struck the crown prince in public, adding with a sneer, 'had I been thus treated by my father, I would have blown my brains out; but this fellow has no honour'. Father

and son were perpetually at loggerheads, the tyrant finally impounding books and flute and forbidding the crown prince to see his mother.

At fifteen years of age Frederick became a major of the Potsdam Guards, a regiment of 2,500 giants, nearly all the rank and file being well above six feet in height. Four years later the crown prince attempted to flee from Prussia, but was arrested and court-martialled. His father overruled the findings and sentence of the court, and had his son's accomplice, a Lieutenant von Katte, executed. The crown prince himself lay imprisoned at Küstrin, apparently in danger of losing his life, and it was only on the intervention of the crowned heads of Europe that he was not executed. His father eventually released and restored him to his rank and position, but only after he had declared himself penitent and willing to submit to his father's direction. And so the son became a liar, a hypocrite, a cynic and a practised dissembler, always hiding his feelings and his thoughts. Henceforth throughout his long life he opened his heart to no man. To please his father he pretended to find fault in his mother and in his

Frederick the Great

favourite sister. Finally, as a reward, he received in 1732 the colonelcy of the von der Goltz Regiment of Infantry and in 1733 a wife, Elizabeth Christina of Brunswick. He wanted neither, but, in the words of one chronicler, 'he retired to the marshy solitudes of Brandenburg to make the best of both'.

For about two years Frederick did little but command his regiment, which he did so well that it gained the approbation of Frederick William. For, after leaving Küstrin, the son devoted himself to work, showing even greater application, energy and method than his father.

In 1734 the king allowed the crown prince to volunteer his services with the Prussian contingent to the imperial army waging war against the French on the Rhine. There Frederick served for a few months under the great Eugene, and he was presumably impressed by him since he took to copying the Supremo's curt speech and abrupt manners. Frederick then returned to his military duties at Ruppin, Reinsberg and Potsdam and, from time to time, undertook duties of state on the king's behalf. Towards the end he appeared to be much attached to his strange and somewhat unnatural father. He had won his father's fullest trust, and Frederick William prophesied of him, '*Da steht Einer, der mich rächen wird.*'

On 31 May 1740, at four in the morning, Frederick William, ailing and sick, rose from his bed for the last time. He awoke his wife, declaring that he was going to die that day. He ordered his horses to be ridden out so that his friends Leopold of Anhalt-Dessau and Hacke, one of his general-adjutants, should each choose one as the king's last gift. Early in the afternoon he died, and his son was immediately proclaimed King Frederick II of Prussia. That evening the Old Dessauer visited the new king, who was sitting in tearful meditation. The old field-marshal voiced his hopes 'that he (the Old Dessauer) would have the same authority as in the late reign'. To which Frederick, twenty-eight years of age, cuttingly replied, 'that he knew of no authority except that of the sovereign king'. And so the Old Dessauer returned home with his gift horse and much on his mind.

Grenadiers of 27 Infantry Regiment (the Old Dessauer's regiment)

The Army

THE INFANTRY

Frederick said in his *Denkwürdigkeiten der Preussischen Geschichte* that Frederick William had wanted to make Prussia a force to be reckoned with in the eyes of its neighbours, for George William's example had taught him how dangerous it was to be defenceless; from his father, King Frederick I, whose troops belonged to his allies (who found their pay) rather than to himself, Frederick William had learned that a monarch is respected in that same measure as his armed might is to be feared. Drawing his conclusions from the humiliations which Frederick I suffered from both Sweden and Russia, when their troops used Prussia's territory much as they pleased, Frederick

15 Infantry Regiment was raised in 1689 from a cadre of 13 Regiment. Up to 1731 it was commanded by von der Goltz who was transferred to 5 Regiment so that Frederick the Crown Prince could take command. Its royal colonel made the regiment's fortune, its first battalion becoming 1 Guard Battalion

William had intended not only to hold Prussia's frontiers firm but to press the Prussian claim to Berg, where the Elector of the Palatine, the last representative of the House of Neuburg, was already near death. 'For the world rested', said Frederick the Great, 'not so firmly on the shoulders of Atlas as the Prussian State on the shoulders of its Army.'

From the beginning of the century the Prussian Army had gained its experience mainly by fighting foreign causes for other nations. It took the field in the Great Northern War (1700–21), and in 1733 sent a 10,000 strong detachment under Lieutenant-General von Röder, as part of the Emperor's forces, to fight the French. But these were only small campaigns compared with the great wars which Frederick II was about to enter, and some of the lessons derived from them, particularly by the Old Dessauer, were to be proved false. The great improvement in Prussian arms from 1713 to 1740 was due not so much to ex-

perience gained on the field as to Frederick William's energy and interest, his eye for detail and his capacity for taking infinite pains in the drilling of his foot soldiers. Nor did his army ever lack money, for, of the total of 7,372,000 thalers annual revenue, 4,900,000 were spent directly on army upkeep and a total of 5,977,000 thalers were allocated to defence. Even so, Frederick William managed his finances so well throughout his twenty-seven year reign that he accrued a reserve of over eight million thalers.

Frederick William's activities as a military administrator covered a very wide field. In 1713 pack horses had been introduced into the Prussian Army to lighten the load of the marching soldier and to carry tents, rather than rely on billetting. The next year a *collegium medicum chirurgicum* was founded to train army surgeons and, since these needed practical experience in their profession, they were affiliated to the newly founded Chante Hospital in Berlin. In 1715 the monarch inaugurated the annual royal review and inspection of his troops, and in the next few years established the Berlin cadet school for officer aspirants, the Spandau and Potsdam arms factories and the Potsdam school for soldiers' orphans. In 1718 he had set up a regional recruiting organization.

What distinguished the Prussian Army of the period from the armies of the other European powers was its discipline and its uniformity. This was principally due to a comprehensive and detailed *Dienst-Reglement*, a form of army standing orders which covered both the performance of duties and the regulations as to discipline and dress, for dress regulations were one of Frederick William's obsessions. Some of the detail of the regulations was taken to a ridiculous extreme; on the other hand every item of the soldier's equipment was designed not merely for appearance and use but also for durability and economy; each piece had a stipulated life before it could be discarded or exchanged. And these orders on dress and duties were strictly enforced. For, as Frederick II said, 'the king mixed freely with his officers, treating his field officers as comrades and his subalterns as though he were their father. And he would have put himself in the guardroom under arrest sooner than appear in a tunic which was not decently turned out and strictly in accordance with regulations.'

The Prussian officer corps, too, differed in many respects from the officer corps elsewhere. Service to the state had been made the compulsory duty of the nobility and this, taking its lead from the monarch, served with dedication. Noblemen from other German states and from abroad were, however, accepted into the Prussian service and some of these foreigners reached the highest ranks. But there was no room for the Prussian middle-class or even the rich merchant in this exclusively noble hierarchy and very little for the soldiers commissioned from the ranks. The Prussian officer corps had become almost a knightly order or military club, where (until 1807) no officer, from Fähnrich to colonel, wore distinguishing badges of rank. Within the Prussian state under Frederick William, the officer began to enjoy both prestige and status, no matter what his rank or financial means.

In 1729 Frederick William put in hand several measures to establish a ready reserve of infantry, by creating a Landmiliz consisting of a number of infantry regiments, each of seven companies, called up for fourteen days training in each year, during which time they received army pay. The regular cadre in each regiment consisted of officers, non-commissioned officers and drummers, often convalescents from regular regiments. This militia formed a partly-trained war-time reserve of reinforcements for the regular forces. Four years later Prussia, with the exception of parts of Westphalia, was divided into war-recruiting and reinforcement Regiment-Cantons, 5,000 house-holds being listed as the recruiting source for a single infantry regiment and 1,800 for a cavalry regiment. To save money, the king also sent numbers of regular infantry regiments on unpaid leave for ten months in the year. It so turned out that this gave rise to civil and military problems which probably outweighed the value of the economies.

Frederick William and the Old Dessauer made a number of improvements in infantry tactics and organization. In 1730 the Old Dessauer invented the iron ramrod for the musket which enabled the rate of infantry fire to be much increased; for the wooden rods used before this

time needed careful handling or they broke in the barrels. The infantry march column and firing line was reduced from four to three ranks, the front rank being trained to fire the musket with the bayonet fixed. That same year, too, saw the introduction in the Prussian Army of marching in step, the rate of step being measured to the minute.

Frederick William kept a close eye on foreign military developments and he usually found a place in the Prussian Army for any newly intro-duced arm, even though he was somewhat un-certain of its benefits and uses. He copied the new fusiliers (armed with the shorter and lighter fusil) from the French, and had originally intended to convert 28 Infantry Regiment to light infantry. But the experiment was not pursued and the fusiliers, except that they wore a fusilier headdress (somewhat shorter than that of the grenadiers) were indistinguishable from the infantry of the line. The last tactical reorganization carried out by royal command was in 1735, when a grenadier company was raised in each infantry battalion. Previous to this time each infantry company had

Fusiliers of 40 and 48 Infantry Regiments

9

its own grenade-throwers, although these could be centralized to form two grenadier platoons which marched at the head of the battalion column. Later, under Frederick II, these grenadier companies were amalgamated to form grenadier battalions.

Frederick William's infantry, at the time of his death, consisted of the foot-guards (Leib-Grenadier-Regiment Nr 6) of three battalions, thirty infantry regiments each of two battalions (except Regiment Nr 3 which had three battalions) and two independent Lilien and Raders battalions, afterwards reformed as Regiment Nr 32. In all there were sixty-six battalions, each consisting of five musketeer companies and one grenadier company, the company having a strength of 120 men.

The value of the troops bequeathed in 1740 by Frederick William to his son varied much by arm. The infantry which formed the bulk of the army was excellent, qualitatively without equal anywhere in the world. And yet, so Frederick II said, even the infantry was already passing its peak for

Musketeers of 13 Infantry Regiment, originally a French regiment raised in 1687 from refugees

lack of use. Ribbons had become obligatory in horses manes; soldiers were being judged by the polished stocks of their muskets rather than by the barrels; pipe-clay was the criterion. 'Any further delay', said Frederick, 'would surely have led to the introduction of rouge and beauty-patches' (*Schminke und Schönpflästerchen*).

THE CAVALRY

Following the example of the Swedes, the main phalanx of European armies had become the heavy cavalry cuirassier, the armoured horseman who decided the issue of the battle by the shock of his charge. The Great Elector had taken great pride in those cuirassiers who had distinguished themselves at Warsaw and Fehrbellin, and this faith in their value had continued up to the time of Frederick William's death when sixty of his 114 cavalry squadrons were of cuirassiers. The cuirassier regiment had five squadrons, the squadron consisting of two companies each of sixty horse.

Yet for some time past, even from the time of the reign of King Frederick I, although the cuirassier was paramount among the cavalry, the emphasis had changed from cuirassier to infantry as a battle-winning arm, and much money had been spent in reforming and re-equipping infantry and artillery at the expense of the horse. This policy was continued by Frederick William and was favoured by the Old Dessauer. The king had been unfavourably impressed by the performance of the imperial cavalry at Malplaquet, where it had been repeatedly driven off; and though he had been present at Menin, Tournai and Stralsund, he had seen no use for cavalry there either. Leopold von Anhalt-Dessau, for his part, could never forgive the failure of the Austrian cavalry of General Styrum, which, in the Old Dessauer's view, was responsible for much of the loss at Hochstädt. And so the prized Prussian infantry assumed its rightful role as the core and phalanx of the army, and it was to prove itself not merely by holding ground against foot and horse, but by breaking the enemy in the shock action of frontal assault by musketry and bayonet.

In addition to the cuirassiers, the Prussian horse in 1740 included twelve regiments of dragoons,

A trooper of von Schorlemmer's Dragoons, Dragoon Regiment No. 6, raised in 1717 from cavalry given to Frederick William I by the King of Poland in exchange for a gift of porcelain

three regiments of ten and three of five squadrons, making forty-five squadrons in all. The dragoon regiments, which owed their origin to the Great Elector, had of course a two-fold role, to fight as cavalry or as infantry. They had distinguished themselves under Derffling, Bomsdorff and Grumbkow at the battles against the Swedes at Rathenow and Fehrbellin, mostly fighting on foot, and in the bloody three-day battle at Warsaw. Under Frederick I and Frederick William, however, they had been neglected in company with the remainder of the Prussian horse. One regiment of dragoons (Regiment Nr 3) had been designated horse grenadier.

One of the fundamental weaknesses of the Prussian cavalry was in the size of its troopers and mounts. For the soldiers were, in the main, big men and, so it was reasoned, they needed big horses to carry them; and they became, in Frederick the Great's words, '*Kolosse auf Elephanten*'. Although bone is of some advantage in the cuirassier charge, it is of course a fallacy to assume that a big horse can travel farther or

faster, clear obstacles better, or necessarily carry more weight, than a smaller animal; for it is breeding and blood which tell. A big horse is certainly less handy, and a light-weight cavalryman is not necessarily at a disadvantage when pitted against a heavy rider, since much depends on the training of both rider and horse. But these truths were not yet known in Prussia in 1740. And so, according to the new king's description, the Prussian cuirassiers and dragoons were not horse masters in any sense of the word. Riders and steeds lacked agility and were unsuited by size, temperament and training to fighting on horseback. They had little eye for country. The dragoons, in particular, could be regarded only as mounted infantry, for they were more at home on the ground than on horseback.

THE HUSSARS

During the eighteenth-century wars in Central Europe, the hussar was to occupy a special place. Originally an irregular light horseman forming part of the Hungarian levies used for border fighting against the Turk, he was usually a small man mounted on a pony and armed with carbine, pistols and sabre. Unlike the uhlan, the Polish border cavalryman, who was more heavily mounted and equipped, very rarely did the hussar carry a lance. Hussars had been introduced into the regular forces of Western and Central Europe through Hungary and Austria, where, according to the claims of their unorthodox leaders, they could be regarded almost as a new mounted arm. For although they could if necessary be used as conventional cavalry to provide shock action, they specialized in deep raiding in the enemy rear, in patrolling and collecting information and, at the same time, in denying the enemy reconnaissance; in addition they provided advance and rear guards and escorts and could undertake the essential police duty of rounding up the many deserters. The uses to which hussars could be put, according to their protagonists, were indeed numerous. The commanders of these new forces were often irregulars or officers of unconventional ideas and background; many of them were Hungarian. In the Austro-Prussian wars the skilful use of mounted troops, and in particular of hussars, whether these formed part of the regular forces or not, was to be of the greatest importance.

In 1721 Frederick William I had come to the conclusion that as the hussar arm was being introduced into other armies in Central and Western Europe, Prussia should not lag behind. The original Prussian establishment was very modest, amounting to no more than thirty hussars under a Captain Schmidt, forming part of von Wuthenow's Dragoner-Regiment Nr 6. This detachment provided the nucleus of what were to become known as the Prussian Hussars, and between 1722 and 1737 they expanded to six squadrons under a Major (later Colonel) Brunikowski, still retaining their affiliation to 6 Dragoon Regiment. Eventually, under Frederick the Great, these squadrons became 1, 3 and 5 Hussar Regiments. In 1740, however, the training of the six squadrons of Prussian Hussars differed little from that of the other line cavalry.

In 1729 Frederick William paid a visit to his married daughter, Wilhelmina, whose husband, the Markgrave of Bayreuth, furnished his father-in-law with an escort of hussars. Frederick William was so impressed by their turn-out and uniforms and by the handiness of their mounts that he decided on his return to Berlin to raise his own personal escort hussar squadron. This was formed the next year, not from Brunikowski's Prussian Hussars, but as a newly raised squadron mounted on greys and recruited by attracting soldiers from Hungary and Bayreuth and from suitable applicants throughout the Prussian cavalry. The new squadron was under von Beneckendorf and one of his two officers was a Lieutenant Hans Joachim von Ziethen (Zieten), a man who was to do much to shape the military fortunes of Prussia.

Von Ziethen had entered the ranks of 24 Infantry Regiment as a volunteer on his fifteenth birthday and from Freicorporal was eventually admitted as a Fähnrich. He was still a Fähnrich at twenty-four years of age, having been passed over repeatedly for promotion to commissioned rank. His colonel, von Schwerin, (the same Schwerin, a veteran of Blenheim, who won Mollwitz and who as a field-marshal was to be cut down on the battlefield of Prague) disliked him 'because of his squeaky voice and mean and in-

In left background an officer of 4 Hussar Regiment. In the foreground a trooper of 3 Dragoon (Schulenburg's) Regiment. This regiment had its distinctive headdress and its designation 'Grenadier zu Pferd' taken from it when, acting as the King's escort, it was routed by Austrian hussars in 1741

significant [*unansehnlich*] appearance'. Zeithen's application to resign was immediately accepted, and he returned home to his father's estate. Three years later, however, he had the fortune to be accepted as a lieutenant in von Wuthenow's 6 Dragoons, which regiment was doubling its establishment of squadrons. There he quarrelled with his squadron commander and was involved twice in duelling escapades, suffering a year's fortress imprisonment for the first and being cashiered for the second. Field-Marshal von Buddenbrock interceded for Ziethen and King Frederick William reluctantly agreed to accept him back into the service and, as he appeared to be an unconventional and difficult officer, had him posted to his own life guard squadron of hussars where a good eye could be kept on him.

Ziethen prospered in the Berlin Hussars, becoming a captain in 1731, and he was attached to the Austro-Hungarian hussars in command of half a squadron of Berlin Hussars and half a squadron of Prussian Hussars in order to gain experience in the new hussar warfare.

Meanwhile the three squadrons of Berlin Hussars had been formed into 2 Hussar Regiment under von Wurm. Ziethen and Wurm were soon at variance, Ziethen challenging his colonel to a duel in which both participants were wounded. Wurm was thought highly of by Frederick William and matters might have gone badly for Ziethen had not the king already been on his death-bed. Shortly afterwards Prussia was at war. Wurm took his regiment into Silesia. But he lacked Ziethen's experience and training in commanding hussars and shortly afterwards Frederick II, dissatisfied with Wurm, replaced him by Ziethen in the command of 2 Hussar Regiment. During the Silesian Wars Ziethen was to win great fame as a leader of cavalry and was to rise rapidly in rank from lieutenant-colonel to general. Many famous Prussian cavalry generals began their service in 2 Hussar Regiment under Ziethen, who held the colonelcy of the regiment from 1741 until 1786, when he died in his eighty-seventh year.

Prussia Challenges Austria

The Habsburg Emperor Charles VI was the Emperor of the Holy Roman Empire but this, as Voltaire said, was neither holy nor Roman, nor even an empire, for it was a traditional relic of the old German Empire of Otto the Great. The imperial title was elective, and although from about 1440 onwards it had become customary to elect a Habsburg to the throne, the electors were always in a position to extort concessions in exchange for their votes; the Habsburgs usually had to grant substantial monetary favours to ensure their own election. The expenses of the imperial crown, which was essentially a German and not an Austrian institution, steadily rose while its power diminished, so that it eventually became only of a traditional prestige importance. Austria itself was an archduchy within the German Empire,

but the Habsburg Emperors were in addition kings of Bohemia and kings of Hungary.

As Holy Roman Emperor, Charles VI had a machinery of government entirely separate from that in Vienna, Prague, Pressburg and Buda. For the imperial government had a diet in Ratisbon representing the members of the three colleges (curiae) of electors, princes and imperial cities, but these were merely debating delegates from independent German states. For in spite of the fact that the 1648 settlement recognized only the territorial supremacy (Landeshoheit) of the rulers, they still enjoyed undisputed and complete sovereignty. The diet concerned itself with little of importance and its decisions had little real effect since there was no means of forcing their implementation. There was no standing imperial defence force, since the existence of such an army depended on contributions from the member states. The empire was divided into ten regions or circles, but across these administrative borders ran a patchwork of more than 300 sovereign German States, large and small. The most important of these, in addition to Austria, were Bavaria, Saxony and Prussia.

Although Brandenburg and East Prussia formed the main component of the Prussian kingdom, Cleves, Mark and Ravensburg, East Pomerania, Halberstadt and Minden were also governed from Berlin. And so it became the ambition of the Brandenburg electors and Prussian kings to unite these many states scattered throughout Germany. Nor could they forget that West Prussia, the Baltic territory between Pomerania and East Prussia and now part of Poland, had once belonged to the Teutonic Order. Frederick William in particular believed that Prussia must expand or stagnate.

The Emperor Charles VI, being without male issue, was concerned that his daughter Maria Theresa should succeed to the Austrian possessions, and in 1728 he asked Frederick William that Prussia should adhere to the Pragmatic Sanction assuring the Austrian female succession. Frederick William's price was the West German Duchy of Berg for Prussia, on the death of its ruler. Spain and Russia were already signatories and Britain and France became additional guarantors a few years later. But having secured signatures from the major European powers, Charles VI had misgivings about his earlier undertaking to support the transfer of Berg to Prussia. Frederick William, nursing a grievance, came to a secret understanding with Austria's traditional enemy France. When Frederick came to the throne shortly afterwards he inherited both the understanding with France and the Prussian hostility to Austria.

A few months later, in October 1740, the Emperor Charles VI died, and his daughter Maria Theresa, a young married woman of twenty-three years, succeeded him. The population of the territories of the Austrian Habsburgs was about twenty-five million, ten million within and fifteen million without the borders of the empire. The young king of Prussia was already preparing to make war on the Habsburgs, a war which was eventually to become the struggle between Prussia and Austria for the mastery of Germany. The population of Prussia and all its dependencies hardly numbered more than four and a half million.

The Prussian Adventurer

When Frederick became king his attitude to his family and the old ministers of state became colder, more withdrawn and more uncivil. He snubbed his mother and sisters and publicly humiliated von der Schulenburg and the Old Dessauer. He began to live behind an impenetrable mask. He was untroubled and uninhibited by conscience, by a standard of common decency, or by any fellow feeling for his brother Germans, inside or outside of Prussia. He was the complete autocrat, friendless, perfidious, irreligious and cynical, the end always justifying the means, ungrateful, avaricious, mistrustful and untrustworthy, the monarch with the perpetual sneer.

Many stories are told about him. And as he was successful and became 'the Great', they were recounted after his death almost with admiration

and affection. He visited the monks of Cleve to find out what they were doing with the revenues of the royal forests made over to them throughout the centuries to pray for the souls of past dukes. Carlyle tells how Frederick asked the purpose of these costly masses. The answer came 'To deliver the souls out of purgatory.' 'Purgatory? It is a costly thing for the forests all this while! And are they not out of purgatory yet, these poor souls, after so many hundred years of praying?' The monks thought not. 'And when will they be out?' The monks could not say. 'Then send me a messenger when it is complete.' And that ended what was to have been a long ceremonial visit, and the king rode off leaving the monks still singing the *Te Deum* with which they had greeted his arrival. When inspecting a prison at Spandau Frederick found only one prisoner who admitted his guilt and the fairness of his sentence, the others maintaining that they were innocent. 'Release the scoundrel immediately', cried the king, 'lest he contaminate all these guiltless people.' On the prompting of the Protestant community at Glogau, he promised the Austrians that he would not use the Protestant church outside the walls as a blockhouse, if they, for their part, would spare it from demolition. But when he had taken Glogau and viewed the church he is said to have cried out, 'What a fearful monstrosity. Of course it must come down!' On seeing a great placard erected by indignant burghers lampooning and criticizing the king for the taxes he had imposed, he merely gave orders that it should be hung lower in order that the people might see it better. During his life-time, however, he was regarded with little affection and the news of his death was received by the Berliners (whom he always disliked) with a sigh of relief.

In the summer of 1740, even before the death of the Emperor Charles VI, the young Frederick was already playing the bully in the Rhineland. He wanted Berg and would have been happy to have Russian or French troops lay waste the Rhineland to help him get it. Like his father, he was tolerant in matters of religion, being content 'that all his subjects should go to heaven in their own way'. But because it politically so suited him, he regarded himself as the champion of all German Protestants. And whereas Frederick William

A drummer and dragoon from 11 Dragoon Regiment, raised in Silesia in 1741 by the Graf von Nassau. The regiment was later destroyed by the Austrians in Moravia

was prepared, if need be, to oppress Prussian Roman Catholics in retaliation for persecution of Protestants by German Roman Catholic rulers elsewhere, his son Frederick II more than hinted that he was ready to go to war on their behalf. In a territorial dispute between the Catholic Archbishop Elector of Mainz and the Protestant Landgrave of Hesse-Cassel, the Archbishop formed a military coalition with the Emperor's support. The Landgrave appealed to Frederick, who wrote to his brother Elector of Mainz saying 'In case of need, we' (that is to say Frederick) 'should not know how to refrain from affording the Landgrave . . . protection and help.' The threat was sufficient to win the day for the Landgrave. The Bishop of Liège left unanswered a Prussian ultimatum and had to buy off the occupying Prussian troops at a price of 200,000 thalers. And the young king, revelling in his own success and jeering at the restraining advice of his own Prussian ministers, said that 'when they talked of war they resembled an Iroquois discussing astronomy'.

When, at the end of October, he learned of the Emperor's death, Frederick had already decided on the seizure of Austrian Silesia. He wanted its rich territory as his price for adherence to the Pragmatic Sanction. The province was contiguous to Brandenburg and brought him further political and strategic advantages in that it cut off the Elector of Saxony, who was also King of Poland, from his territories in the east. Silesia outflanked Western Poland, also coveted by Frederick. Prussia had of course no moral or legal right to the territory. And when his minister Podewils urged that some pretext or claim be furbished up, the king replied, 'That is what *you* are for. The orders have already been given out to the troops.' On 9 November Frederick received news of the death of the Empress of Russia and, having nothing more to fear on his eastern flank, this confirmed him in his intention to occupy Silesia, come what may.

The Prussian preparations had been made in the greatest of secrecy, all activity being cloaked in the guise of a march to be made to the west to secure the provinces of Jülich-Berg on the Rhine, those provinces already promised to Frederick William. By the end of November, however, the British Ambassador was already convinced that

Von Pomeiske's 9 Dragoon Regiment originally raised by von Platen in 1727

Silesia was the goal, and Vienna, suddenly awakening to the danger, sent the Marquis di Botta on a special mission to Berlin to inquire the Prussian intentions. Di Botta *en route* had passed great columns of Prussians already moving south and it was no longer possible for Frederick to dissemble. He openly laid claim to Silesia, in return for which he promised support for Maria Theresa and her husband's claim to the imperial throne. Both men threatened, the Austrian envoy leaving with the reminder that 'though the Prussian troops make a handsomer show than the Austrian, ours have smelt powder'. In early December Prussian troops crossed into Silesia.

Frederick rightly judged Austro-Hungary, in spite of its size and large population, to be disunited and militarily weak, and he was correct in believing that the political climate in Europe was auspicious for an unprovoked attack. He was wrong, however, in his assessment of the energy, strength and wisdom of the new Austrian ruler, by far the most distinguished monarch the Habsburgs ever produced, and in the fervent support she was to receive as Queen of Hungary from the Hungarian people.

The War of the Austrian Succession, insofar as it concerns operations in Central Europe, embraces what is usually referred to as the First and Second Silesian Wars.

The First Silesian War

The command of the main Prussian force, 28,000 strong, which had been under von Schwerin, passed to Frederick as soon as he joined the field army, while the hereditary Prince of Anhalt-Dessau (the Young Dessauer) was to follow from Berlin with a reserve of 12,000 men. The Austrian troops in Silesia were unprepared for battle and numbered only 600 horse and 3,000 foot. Their military governor, von Wallis, a soldier of Scottish descent, was soon locked up commanding a siege

A drummer of von Krockow's 2 Dragoon Regiment, originally raised in 1725

force of 1,000 Austrians in Glogau. Wallis's deputy, von Browne, a German-Irish Roman Catholic, who happened to be in the south of Silesia at the time, began to draw in detachments from Moravia, but these he dissipated by allocating them to fortresses and strongholds, while keeping only 600 dragoons under his own hand.

There was a large Protestant element among the German population of Silesia and this welcomed Frederick in his newly assumed role of Protestant protector; the Roman Catholics were passive. And so, in spite of very bad weather, the Prussians advanced steadily through the flooded countryside in two columns, Frederick with the larger and Schwerin with the smaller, the town of Liegnitz being taken by Schwerin by a *coup de main*. By the end of January most of Silesia had been occupied without serious fighting, although Glogau, Brieg and Neisse still held out.

Frederick regarded the war as over since Silesia was already his, and he returned to Berlin to patch up a peace through diplomatic channels. There he learned to his chagrin that the Austrians were mobilizing in earnest. France, anxious for a share in the spoils, was demanding the Austrian

Netherlands and Luxembourg, while the Elector of Bavaria was claiming the imperial throne. Franco-Bavarian troops were preparing to invade Austria and Bohemia, while England and Holland, siding against the French, were sending a subsidy to Vienna.

Frederick was obliged to set out again immediately for Silesia where the once favourable military situation was rapidly deteriorating. The two Austrian generals, Browne and Lentulus, had turned Glatz into a military base and were infiltrating both regular and partisan troops back into Silesia. About 600 men had forced their way through the blockading Prussians and reinforced the Austrian garrison at Neisse. The Silesian roads and backwoods had become infested with irregulars, both foot and horse, principally Hungarian

and Croat pandours and Magyar irregular hussars. In Prussian eyes the pandour-hussars were indisciplined predators, but they gave endless trouble, cutting off detachments and murdering the wounded. Indeed they were so bold that they would hang about the Prussian encampments in broad daylight just outside musket range, watching and reporting all movement and activity. They were no match for disciplined Prussian infantry, but so great was the self-esteem of the Magyar irregular hussars that they were not afraid to attack Prussian cavalry, for they were better horsemen and their mounts were handier and more agile. At Baumgarten they attacked the king's escort of Schulenburg Dragoons and put it to flight and Frederick himself barely escaped capture.

The Battlefields of the Silesian Wars
Brandenburg, Silesia and Bohemia-Moravia

An officer of 3 Dragoon Regiment (originally von der Schulenburg's Dragoons)

These hussars and pandours, in spite of their indiscipline, were excellent in tying down garrisons and in collecting information and denying the enemy reconnaissance. Even in those areas where the population was Protestant and friendly to the king it became difficult for the Prussians to learn what was going on in Silesia. Beyond the borders it was impossible. When a new Austrian army under Neipperg (Neuperg) entered Silesia on its way to relieve the garrison at Neisse, the Austrian field-marshal, in the words of one chronicler, 'walked invisible within clouds of pandours'.

Frederick, by good fortune, first heard of Neipperg's approach from Austrian deserters. Glogau had already been taken by the Young Dessauer in a night action. The Brieg blockade was given up and Frederick prepared to meet the oncoming Austrians.

MOLLWITZ AND CHOTUSITZ

Mollwitz was Frederick's first battle and there the greatest warrior of his age made a most unpromising beginning. Although the season was late (it was nearly mid-April) there were days of raging snowstorms, which at times cut visibility down to twenty yards, and nearly two feet of snow lay on the ground. Neipperg should have known of Frederick's whereabouts since mounted pandours had captured or shot down all the Prussian messengers sent by Frederick to bring up reinforcements. Frederick certainly did not know where the Austrians were, although in fact they lay only seven miles away, until he heard the news, so it is said, almost by accident from a Silesian farm labourer at daybreak on the morning of 10 April. A quick march brought him to the village of Mollwitz where he surprised the Austrians at their dinner.

How Neipperg allowed the Prussians to approach unobserved is not known, but no cavalry screen appeared to have been posted until the firing of outpost rockets warned Neipperg that something was afoot. A hussar party was then sent out but this came galloping back with Prussian dragoons at their heels. Neipperg called for Römer, his Saxon General of Horse, the alarm was sounded and the troops sent for from the outlying villages.

Frederick had allocated six squadrons of dragoons and three of hussars to the command of Colonel Graf von Rothenburg, a soldier of fortune with a remarkable record. Born in Polnisch-Retkau, he had joined the French Army in 1727 but, five years later, he transferred to the Spanish service and saw action in Morocco. He returned to his French regiment, of which he became colonel, before entering the Prussian Army in the same rank in 1740. According to German chroniclers it was due to von Rothenburg's skilful handling of horse that the Prussian infantry were able to deploy undisturbed. Be that as it may, Frederick deployed his infantry in two lines about 300 yards apart, each line being made up of three ranks. The first line was commanded by von Schwerin and the second by the Young Dessauer, with Frederick himself in overall command. The cavalry were divided on both wings with some grenadier battalions to give them some stiffening. The Prussians had over 20,000 men on the field of which about 4,000 were cavalry, and over sixty guns. The Austrians totalled somewhat less and had only eighteen guns, but their cavalry strength was double that of the Prussian.

At two in the afternoon the Prussian guns opened a sustained fire on the Austrian left wing made up of Römer's horse and soon inflicted many casualties. The Austrian cavalry became restless and then angry, demanding to be led forward into the attack. Neipperg was two miles away on the right still bringing troops on to the field. Römer could get no orders and finally, unable to hold his men back any longer, he gave the order for his thirty squadrons to advance and then to charge. The Prussian cavalry on the right were swept away and fled between its now lines of infantry, hotly pursued by Römer's Austrians. Nine guns were taken and the two Prussian lines were soon enveloped in a sea of white-coated cavalry. It looked as if the Prussians had already lost their first battle.

Some say that the fleeing Prussian horse swept Frederick away with them. But it seems that the king considered the battle irretrievably lost. Schwerin confirmed his fears although he considered that 'there might still be a chance' of holding. Others say that Schwerin begged the king to flee rather than become a prisoner. Whatever the circumstances, flee he certainly did,

An officer of 8 Cuirassier Regiment, a Brandenburg regiment which, although dating as cuirassiers only from 1734, owed its origin to Brandenburg-Bayreuth cavalry of 1690

leaving von Schwerin, a veteran of Blenheim, in command. Frederick galloped off to Oppeln, thirty-five miles in the rear to cross the Oder by the bridge there, but when he arrived he found that Austrian hussars and pandours had reached the bridge before him. Some of his party were killed or captured as they wheeled about and set off back again for the doubtful safety of Mollwitz, the Austrian horse being in close pursuit.

Meanwhile at Mollwitz Schwerin had sent a messenger to the Young Dessauer, in command of the second line, ordering him to hold, come what may. The Young Dessauer, who disliked Schwerin, sent back a tart rejoinder that he knew where his duty lay and required none save the king to remind him of it. The two lines of Prussian infantry, extending over a frontage of about a mile and a half, separated though they were, still held their ground stoutly, pouring volley after volley into the Austrian horse which repeatedly came back to the charge. On the flanks the grenadier battalions, deserted by the Prussian horse, stood in the enemy midst like little islands. Yet few of the Prussians had been in action before. By evening Römer and Göldlein, the Austrian commander of infantry on the left flank, were dead. The Austrian horse, shot through by musketry, were tired and dispirited at their failure to break the enemy line; after the fifth charge they refused to advance again. Compared with the Prussian, the Austrian infantry were poorly trained in musketry, and without iron ramrods could deliver only two rounds to the Prussian five. Within Prussian musket range, the Austrians could not stand their ground.

At seven in the evening, as the sun was setting, Schwerin sensed that the advantage had passed to him; he ordered a general advance, and the Austrians sullenly trooped off the field. There was no pursuit. Thus ended the battle of Mollwitz, the Prussian casualties being 4,600 dead, wounded and missing against an Austrian loss of 4,400.[1]

Thereafter Frederick was never to allude to his own flight but was to hold a secret grievance against Schwerin. The king had been surprised at the steadfastness of the Austrian troops who had been outnumbered by better equipped and better trained infantry; he was quick to recognize, too, the inferiority of the Prussian horse. And so he began the systematic retraining of Prussian cavalry.

Maria Theresa, anxious to start operations against the Franco-Bavarians, had, much against her will, begun negotiations with Frederick. Frederick and Neipperg met in secrecy and by the Convention of Klein Schnellendorf, Frederick played false to his allies, agreeing to conduct sham skirmishes and sieges in order to deceive the French. In reality he was to withdraw Prussia from the war, leaving the Austrians free to clear Bohemia of the enemy. In return Frederick demanded that he retain his Silesian spoils. At first, however, the Austrians had no success and the Franco-Bavarian troops had little difficulty in overrunning Bohemia, so that Frederick, incensed by jealousy and surprised at what he believed to be the Austrian weakness, went back on his secret agreement and ordered the occupation of Glatz and Moravia. But once in Moravia, Frederick received little help from the French who soon withdrew. The Slovak inhabitants were hostile

The Household Troops in dress uniform; an ADC, and officers of the Garde-du-Corps and the Gens d'armes Cuirassiers

and the pandours were everywhere, giving the Saxons in particular a rough handling. Frederick was unable to take Brünn and the Saxons departed for home, this causing a permanent breach in the Prusso-Saxon alliance. The discomfited Frederick was forced to retire to Bohemia where he was met at Chotusitz by a 30,000 strong Austrian Army under Charles of Lorraine.

The battle of Chotusitz was fought on 17 May 1742. The village of Chotusitz itself was held by the Young Dessauer while Frederick was to the right with the foot grenadiers, the horse and much of the artillery. The sequence of the battle was at first very much the same as at Mollwitz, with the Prussian artillery playing on the Austrian cavalry flank, with the difference, however, that it was the Prussian horse which first rode into the attack and the Austrian cavalry which gave way. The Austrian infantry in the centre, little daunted, marched straight into Chotusitz where the broken ground and ditches made it impossible for Frederick's cavalry to penetrate. The battle was of the fiercest, the Austrians fighting not with their customary obstinacy but with fury. But they lost the day and nearly half their men. The belief took hold, not only abroad but in Vienna, that the Prussians were invincible.[2]

A negro or Moor drummer-boy of 19 Infantry Regiment, formed in 1702 from cadres of 4, 6, 7 and 11 Regiments. Numbers of Moors were used as musicians

Maria Theresa sued for peace and the Treaty of Berlin in July 1742 marked the end of the First Silesian War. Saxony went out of the war with Prussia. Austro-Hungarian troops then cleared Bohemia of the French and invaded Bavaria, driving the Elector, who had meanwhile been crowned as Holy Roman Emperor, from his own Munich capital. France was forced back on the defensive, having lost the battle of Dettingen, and Maria Theresa prepared to invade Alsace.

None of this was to Frederick's liking, for he had no wish to see France forced out of the war, since this would, he believed, leave him alone to face Austria; he suspected that Maria Theresa's cession of Silesia was merely an arrangement of convenience until Bavaria, France and Spain were beaten. Frederick hastened to ally himself once more to France, Bavaria, the Palatine and Hesse-Cassel. As soon as the Austrian forces had entered Alsace, Frederick ordered the invasion of Bohemia.

The Second Silesian War

On August 1744 Frederick set 80,000 Prussians on the march towards Prague and held a further 20,000 in reserve in Silesia. Prague fell in September. Frederick, Schwerin and the Young Dessauer continued their triumphant progress towards Tabor and Austria.

Maria Theresa, however, had been to Pressburg once more to appeal to the Hungarian nation for help. Charles of Lorraine had been ordered to quit Alsace and bring his army eastwards. With the arrival in Bohemia of the Hungarian horse and pandours, Prussia's fortune soon changed, for the Magyars insolently enclosed encampments and columns, controlled the highways and captured all messengers, so that for a whole month Frederick was out of touch with his kingdom and the rest of Europe, with no news of friend or foe. On 19 November he was attacked

by Austrians and Saxons and was forced to retreat out of Bohemia with a heavy loss of equipment. The Austrians then invaded Bavaria once more and prepared to re-enter Silesia.

HOHENFRIEDBERG AND SOHR

Prince Charles of Lorraine crossed into Silesia with more than 60,000 men, of which about a third were Saxons. By the clever use of an unsuspecting double spy Frederick had led Charles to believe that if Silesia were entered, the Prussians would behave as they had done in 1744, that is to say retreat to the north to avoid being cut off from Breslau. To reinforce this idea in Charles's mind Frederick evacuated part of the south-east. In fact, the king intended to take the offensive with a force of 70,000 men as soon as the Austrian enemy could be lured down into the Silesian plain.

The battle took place between Hohenfriedberg and Striegau, beyond which the Prussian forces lay hidden. On the previous night the Prussians had been brought forward and deployed, and they attacked the Saxon advance guard at daybreak on 4 June 1745. Charles of Lorraine was still in bed and by the time he roused himself the engagement was half lost. Once more the Prussian infantry showed itself to be superior to the Austrian in training and musketry, and the

A medical officer tending a wounded hussar of Werner's 6 Hussar Regiment

Cavalry officers (3, 1 and 8 Hussars) and, background right, of 5 Dragoon Regiment

Frederick, while a great force of pandours fell on the Prussian baggage, the wild Croats murdering all in their path, women as well as men. But the arrival of the Austrian main force was an hour too late and its movement was detected at daybreak by Prussian outposts. Frederick and his staff were already up and at work, and the Prussian reactions, as usual, were much quicker than those of the Austrian.

On the Austrian left wing were twenty-eight guns and fifty squadrons of horse; the guns opened fire but the horse and infantry stood immobile whereas, as Frederick said later, 'they should have thundered down on us'. Turning to the colonel of 1 Cuirassiers, Frederick is reported to have said, 'Here you, Buddenbrock, get into them with your cuirassiers.' The cuirassiers galloped uphill, but met no counter-charge, 'merely the crackle of carbines'. The Austrian cavalry wing was swept away. The Prussian foot on the right, following up the cuirassiers, climbed the slope, losing heavily in the case-shot fire which raked them. The Prussians threw in their three reserve regiments of infantry. The guns were taken and the enemy driven off. Frederick then

Austrian horse was unwilling to close with the Prussian new model cavalry. By eight o'clock that morning Charles ordered a retreat and the columns pulled back covered by rearguards. The Prussian loss had been 5,000; that of the Austrians and Saxons 9,000 dead and wounded, 7,000 prisoners and 66 cannon. A further 8,000 deserted. Frederick claimed that there had not been so great a victory since Blenheim.[3] The Prussians followed up the Austrian army, now reduced to about 40,000, moving into north-east Bohemia to eat the country bare.

At the end of September Frederick, so troubled by pandours on his line of communications that 11,000 horse and foot had to be detached to guard ration convoys, began to fall back towards Silesia, crossing the Elbe and encamping with 18,000 men at the foot of the mountains near the village of Sohr (Soor).

Charles of Lorraine, following in the wake of the Prussians with an army of 30,000, had determined to make a surprise night attack on the Prussian camp. On the night of 29 September, after a clever approach march in the dark, the Austrian force arrived on the high ground above

A chaplain upbraiding drunken looters of the Frei-Corps. Left, a grenadier of von Shorny's Corps and, right, two Croat hussars of von Kleist's Cavalry

A trooper of Frei-Husar, originally raised in 1759 in Saxony by von Kleist, the Colonel of 1 Hussar Regiment

returned to Silesia to lay astride the Austrian approach route. On 23 November Prussian forward elements, light horse, cuirassiers and foot, were in contact with uhlans of Charles of Lorraine's Saxon advance guard. There, at Hennersdorf, Ziethen, who was in command, destroyed the 6,000 strong Saxon force of horse and foot under von Buchner.[5] Surprise having been lost, Charles turned in his tracks and returned to Bohemia. And so the whole enterprise collapsed.

Frederick now invaded Saxony. The Old Dessauer moved from Halle to Leipzig and then began a march towards Dresden, throwing a bridge over the Elbe so that Frederick, coming up from Silesia, might join him. A Saxon force under Rutowski, including an Austrian contingent, lay west of the Saxon capital. Charles of Lorraine was marching out of Bohemia with 46,000 men, in order to aid his Saxon ally. Frederick goaded on the Old Dessauer to attack the Saxons before Charles should join them, and not wait for Frederick's own arrival. When the Old Dessauer did give battle on 15 December, Charles of Lorraine was not five miles away.

transferred the remainder of his cavalry to his left wing where the two lines still stood apart. Again the Austrian horse on that wing broke, leaving bare the infantry flank. The Austrians poured back into the forest where the Prussian cavalry could no longer pursue. Meanwhile the pandours in the rear, fully engaged in looting, brought no aid to the main battle. The engagement cost the Austrians 4,000 dead and wounded and 3,000 prisoners. The Prussian loss was about 4,000.[4]

HENNERSDORF
AND KESSELSDORF

Because Frederick was certain that the Austrians must be forced to come to terms he ordered his army to withdraw slowly into Silesia, while he himself returned to Berlin. His own army was dispersed into winter quarters and he assumed that the Austrian would do the same.

Meanwhile, however, the Austrians and Saxons had drawn up a plan to invade Brandenburg that winter and take Berlin; but the details of the campaign came to Frederick's ears and he

The standard bearer of the Garde-du-Corps, first formed as a squadron in 1740. It formed the heavy cavalry personal escort for the King and was numbered as 13 Cuirassier Regiment

On 15 December 1745, at Kesselsdorf, the Old Dessauer attacked the entrenched Saxon force, the Prussian infantry marching uphill through wet snow against the massed fire of 9,000 muskets and thirty guns. The Prussian cavalry hung about on the outskirts. Time after time the Prussians fell back, their ranks shot through, amid fearful casualties. An Austrian battalion, seeing the Prussian infantry near disintegration, left its entrenchments in pursuit and was followed by the Saxon foot. There in the open they were cut to pieces by the Prussian horse. Rutowski lost the battle: 3,000 dead and wounded and nearly 7,000 prisoners.[6] The Prussians lost 4,600 men but at long last gained the peace. For Charles of Lorraine turned back yet again into Bohemia.

This ended the Second Silesian War and, by the Treaty of Dresden signed on Christmas Day, Austria was forced to agree to Silesia remaining in Prussian hands. Frederick, for his part, acknowledged Maria Theresa's husband, Francis Stephen, as Emperor. Prussia, often faced with disaster, had been saved by Frederick's audacity and military skill.

The war between Austria and France continued for yet another three years in the Netherlands and Italy, peace being finally made at Aix-la-Chapelle in 1748. The astute Maria Theresa, distrustful of Frederick, resentful at the loss of Silesia and disappointed in Britain's effort as Austria's ally during the war, looked about her for new allies against the resumption of the struggle.

Frederick's New Model Army

Frederick had depended for his early successes on the magnificent infantry bequeathed to him by his father, Frederick William. And almost immediately after his succession, Frederick II himself began to reform and expand the Prussian foot to almost twice its original establishment.

His first measure, customary after any change

A hussar-trumpeter wearing the distinctive trumpeter's headdress

of Prussian sovereign, was the reorganization of the foot guards. The giant Potsdam Guard (Infanterie Regiment Nr 6) so beloved by his father, was virtually disbanded, being reformed as a single grenadier guard battalion; the remainder were paid off or transferred to Prince Henry of Prussia's newly raised Infanterie Regiment Nr 35 and Garnison-Bataillon Nr 4. Frederick's own Regiment Nr 15 (formerly Regiment von der Goltz) became the new regiment of royal foot guards. To this guard Frederick added another mounted regiment of guards, the Garde-du-Corps, cuirassiers who eventually took precedence as 13 Cuirassier Regiment.

From 1740 onwards Frederick raised a series of new infantry regiments; in 1740 Musketier-Regiment Nr 34, and Füsilier-Regimenter 33, 35, 36, 37, 38, 39, 40; in 1741, Füsilier-Regimenter Nr 41, 42, 43 and, in 1742 and 1743, Füsilier-Regimenter Nr 45, 46, 47, 48. No further field infantry regiments were formed (with the exception of 49 which was in reality an engineer regiment) until 1772–74 when a single Musketier-Regiment Nr 50 and five Füsilier-Regimenter (Nr 51–55) came into being.

1 Horse Grenadier, von der Schulenburg's Regiment, summer field service uniform, 1729-41
2 Grenadier, Grenadier Guard Battalion No. 6, summer field service uniform, c. 1745
3 Grenadier, von Arnim Regiment (5 Infantry Regiment), summer field service uniform, c. 1729

Michael Youens

A

Trooper, von Ruesch's Death's-Head Hussars (5 Hussar Regiment),
summer field service uniform, c. 1744

Michael Youens

1 Lieutenant, von Dewitz's Hussars
  (1 Hussar Regiment), parade and
  summer field service uniform, c. 1748
2 Musketeer, von Forcade's Regiment
  (23 Infantry Regiment), summer field service uniform, c. 1756
3 Bombardier, Prussian Artillery,
  field service uniform, c. 1750

Michael Youens

C

1 Freijäger, De le Noble'sches Freicorps,
  summer field service uniform, 1756-63
2 Bosniak Lancer, Bosnian Corps,
  summer dress, c. 1760
3 Grenadier, von Schony's Freicorps,
  summer uniform, c. 1761

Michael Youens

Trooper, von Vippach's Hussars (4 Hussar Regiment),
summer field service order, c. 1752

Michael Youens

E

1 Drummer, von Below's Regiment
  (11 Infantry Regiment), summer field
  service uniform *c.* 1757
2 Grenadier, von Canitz Regiment
  (2 Infantry Regiment), summer field
  service order, *c.* 1762
3 Dragoon, von Gschray's Freicorps,
  summer field service order, *c.* 1761

F

Michael Youens

1 and 2 **Officer and Grenadier,**
1 Battalion of the Guard (No. 15),
summer parade uniform, *c.* 1786
3 **Officer, Garde-du-Corps, ceremonial**
guard dress (*Galawachtanzug***),** *c.* 1786

1 Non-commissioned officer, Miner Corps,
winter field service dress, *c.* 1792
2 Infantry Regimental Quartermaster,
winter uniform, *c.* 1761
3 Supply Detail, Commissariat
(*Proviantknecht*), winter uniform, *c.* 1756

H

Michael Youens

From a painting of Major-General Paul von Werner, the colonel in chief of 6 Hussar Regiment from 1757–1785

In addition there were twelve garrison regiments of infantry which, although designed to defend fortresses, were sometimes used as field infantry. Between 1742 and 1753 six independent grenadier battalions were raised (numbered from one to six), these being additional to the twenty-five grenadier battalions formed by detaching the two grenadier companies from each line regiment; these grenadier battalions were not numbered but were usually designated by the names of their commanders.[7]

Frederick made some use of light infantry Jäger or Scharfschützen, although he was not the first to introduce them, for they had been from time to time in the Prussian service since 1656. In 1740, however, he re-introduced them as a corps of guides, at first only a half-company strong, recruited from hunters and gamekeepers. By 1760 the corps had reached a strength of 800. Too often, however, the Jäger were misused as regular infantry, and the larger part of the corps was virtually destroyed near Spandau holding unfavourable open country against Russian Cossacks. In 1763 the corps was reformed at a strength of 300 men, but not till 1787, the year following the formation of the first Jägerregiment, was every Jäger equipped with a rifled carbine. In all, the dismounted Jäger had little military significance during the Silesian Wars and his latter-day role was undertaken by hussars and the numerous Frei Korps. Side by side with the Jäger zu Fuss was the Feldjäger-Corps zu Pferde, also recruited from foresters, which was, however, designed not for fighting but for conducting the courier and field postal service.

Although Frederick much increased the establishment of his infantry and was later to vary its tactics, he did little to alter its organization. It was a different story with the Prussian line cavalry which had shown itself so unsatisfactory at Mollwitz. Except for the new guard regiment, the Garde-du-Corps, no further cuirassier regiments were raised, but Frederick did bring into being a further five dragoon regiments (8–12 Dragoons). These took their place beside the cuirassiers in providing the shock action to break the Austrian horse.

The Silesian Wars, as we have already said, were in some respects revolutionary wars in that they introduced new tactics and new types of troops; very mobile light cavalry and partisans and pandours, Magyar irregular hussars and Croat light horse, the Polish uhlan and the Saxon lancer. At first the Prussian cavalry of the line was quite unfitted to cope with these enemies and success only came with the expansion of the Prussian hussar arm. When Frederick II ascended the throne he possessed only nine squadrons of hussars, but between 1741 and 1773 he added to this number a further eighty-one German and nine Bosnian squadrons, eventually forming Husar-Regimenter Nr 3–10. None of Frederick's cavalry, except for the Bosnian hussars, carried the lance.

Maria Theresa had made excellent use of the scores of bands of irregulars raised as Frei Korps by Austrian and Hungarian soldiers of fortune. These relied for payment on booty and loot. Many were no more than bloodthirsty criminals who terrorized friend and foe alike. Yet it proved impossible to combat them by the formal military methods of the time. In spite of the obvious advantages which the use of the Frei Korps brought to their paymasters, for although difficult to con-

Hussars of the Leib-Husaren Korps and the Magdeburg Husaren Korps

to the regiment. Field artillerymen, whether Kanoniere or Bombardiere, formed the gun crews for the three distinct branches of artillery, Fortress Artillery, Regimental Artillery and Battery Artillery.

Regimental Artillery consisted of those guns decentralized to the infantry, usually two three-pounder or four-pounder guns to each infantry battalion. After 1756 these infantry pieces were replaced by the heavier six-pounder. The gun detachment of two guns might be commanded by a Feuerwerker, Sergeant, Corporal or Bombardier, and each gun crew consisted of two artillery soldiers reinforced by infantrymen or men from the Handlanger service. Battery Artillery (or Positions-Geschützen) formed the main bulk of the artillery which was fought by centralized batteries. At the beginning of the Silesian Wars it totalled only sixty guns.[8] By 1758 this number had been increased to over 200 pieces, and a year later the total count of battalion and battery guns was 580.

Frederick the Great had been much impressed in 1757 with the performance of Russian horse artillery, particularly in the close fire support it

trol they were cheap to maintain and they were particularly effective in denying access, supplies and intelligence to the enemy, Frederick at first refused to use Prussian raised Frei Korps and placed his hopes on regular hussars, both to penetrate the enemy rear and, at the same time, combat the enemy Frei Korps. When the war broke out again in 1756, however, the king did not hesitate to commission Prussian and foreign officers, gentlemen, adventurers and freebooters to raise 'free' regiments, battalions and companies of both horse and foot. About forty-five different formations or units were listed on the rolls. Most of them wore their own distinctive uniform, for they were generally better disciplined and equipped than their Austrian counterparts.

In 1740 the Prussian field artillery had consisted of only six companies but the next year the establishment was almost doubled when Frederick formed the earlier companies into 1 Field Artillery Regiment, at the same time raising a second regiment (Nr 2) of five Kanonier companies and one Bombardier company. By 1762 the total order of battle had been raised to thirty companies, with five companies to the battalion and three battalions

A trooper, non-commissioned officer, trumpeter and officer from 1 Hussar Regiment, formerly the Prussian Hussars

had given to Russian cavalry. Two years later he introduced it into the Prussian service. The first batteries consisted of ten six-pounders each drawn by a team of six horses, but these were later replaced by the lighter three-pounders and four-horse teams.

Engineers, pontoniers and miners formed a very small auxiliary corps under Frederick William. During Frederick's reign the engineer corps was developed into the main technical corps responsible for the direction of pioneers, pontoniers and miners; its establishment consisted entirely of officers and warrant officers (forty-eight officers and thirteen conductors in 1786). Previous to the expansion of this corps the two companies of miners, ten companies of pioneers and the pontoniers had been the general responsibility of the artillery.

The Seven Years War

Frederick's insulting raillery had made enemies of the French king and the Russian empress, and his clumsy attempt to destroy Anglo-Russian accord had drawn Russia, Austria and France in league against him. Russia, Austria and Saxony were openly hostile to Prussia. Frederick feared the Russian, so he said, more than he feared God and, being aware that Elisabeth and her minister Count Bestuzhin-Ryumin were bitterly anti-Prussian, he had good reason to expect a joint Austro-Russian attack on East Prussia and Silesia. And, since he had a standing army of 150,000 men and fourteen million thalers put aside for a new war, he resolved, without consulting his only ally, Britain, to make an unprovoked and pre-emptive attack on Austria by invading Saxony. The Seven Years War, sometimes known as the Third Silesian War, was a resumption of the struggle for the retention of Silesia and the mastery of the German Empire. For Frederick it was a war of survival for, if Prussia failed, it would be dis-

membered by the powerful coalition which faced it.

Frederick lay siege to the Saxon army in the mountainous region of Pirna, where it put up an unexpectedly tough resistance. Frederick succeeded, however, in repelling the Austrian attempts at relief and finally starved the force into submission. He then incorporated the whole of the Saxon force into the Prussian Army, replacing the Saxon officers by Prussians. Saxony itself remained in Prussian occupation for nearly six years.

Yet Frederick had made a poor beginning to the war. The German Protestant rulers were, admittedly, generally sympathetic to him but, in the face of Austrian diplomacy, his position was rapidly deteriorating. Russia had agreed to enter the war against Prussia in return for an Austrian subsidy. Maria Theresa offered to trade the Austrian Netherlands to France and Spain in exchange for their active participation in the war and the return of Silesia to Austria. Sweden entered the war against Prussia.

PRAGUE, KOLIN AND GROSS-JÄGERNDORF

In the spring of 1757 Frederick invaded Bohemia with four columns, three from Saxony and a fourth, under Schwerin, from Silesia. About 60,000 Austrians under Charles of Lorraine were concentrated in the neighbourhood of Prague, waiting for the arrival of Daun with a further 30,000 troops. Frederick was determined to rout Charles before Daun should join him and, against Schwerin's wishes and advice, he ordered the 64,000 tired Prussians to attack on 6 May the entrenched positions east of the Bohemian capital.

Frederick made the mistake of ordering an attack across ground which had not been reconnoitred; what Frederick had taken for lush water meadows were in fact carp ponds, two to three feet deep, covered with water weed. When the Prussian infantry arrived at the carp ponds they were met by the tearing fire of artillery case-shot at 400 paces. They stormed the batteries but were then thrown out by Austrian grenadiers. Schwerin, seventy-three years old, was killed there. The Prussians were left in possession of the battlefield but the Austrians fell back into Prague in good

A hussar of 7 Hussar Regiment in close combat with a dismounted Hungarian hussar or pandour

order. Frederick put his loss at 18,000 men and he bemoaned 'that this day saw the pillars of the Prussian infantry cut down'.[9]

Frederick spent a month unsuccessfully besieging the Bohemian capital and then set out in search of what he imagined was easier prey, the 30,000-strong army of Field-Marshal von Daun which lay astride the Prague-Vienna highway near Kolin. In fact Daun was much more powerful than the Prussians imagined him to be and he had taken up a strongly entrenched position overlooking the main road. Ziethen's advance guard of horse and foot ran into a trap and was separated from the main battle; the Hungarian and Croat skirmishers were most troublesome to the undeployed Prussian columns, and Frederick was eventually forced to attack uphill over ground of Daun's choosing. The battle, which had raged to and fro for hours, was finally decided by the Austrian horse which scattered the Prussian foot. The total Austrian loss was only 8,000; the Prussian casualties included 8,000 dead, 6,000 prisoners and 45 cannon lost.[10] Frederick had been decisively beaten and he had to quit Bohemia. Pomerania and East Prussia had been invaded by Swede and Russian.

At the end of August the Russian Field-Marshal Apraxin (Apraksin) at the head of 80,000 men, having laid waste to the borderlands of East Prussia, attacked half that number of Prussians under Lehwald. At Gross-Jägerndorf on 30 August after a ten hour battle Lehwald was beaten, losing nearly 5,000 men and twenty-seven guns. It was claimed that the Russian casualties were about 9,000.[11] Maria Theresa's forces spilled over into Silesia and an Austrian cavalry and partisan force under General Haddik, 15,000 strong, raided Berlin and extracted from the capital a ransom of a quarter of a million thalers. Frederick's fortunes were at a low ebb.

THE PRUSSIAN RECOVERY

Frederick survived the summer and autumn of 1757 because of the lack of co-ordination between his enemies. The Russians, believing that the Empress Elisabeth was dead, withdrew out of East Prussia behind the Niemen. The French force in Hanover remained inactive. In Lusatia, Daun and Prince Charles had out-manoeuvred a Prussian force under the king's brother, Augustus William, but, in spite of Maria Theresa's urging, they would not come to grips with the enemy.

By November 1757, however, it looked as if the French were going over to the offensive when an army under Soubise began to march through Thuringia on Saxony, joining up with an Austro-Saxon force. The allies numbered about 50,000 men. Frederick made haste to meet them.

Soubise was contemptuous of Prussian arms and was obsessed with the idea that Frederick was in retreat and might escape him. He undertook a clumsy manoeuvre to outflank the Prussians and get across their line of withdrawal; in the course of it he was himself surprised and taken in the flank when still in column of march. There at Rossbach, on the afternoon of 5 November 1757, von Seydlitz's thirty-eight squadrons of horse, with infantry and guns in support, hit the Franco-Austrian column. By four o'clock the French were in full flight, leaving 3,000 dead and wounded and 5,000 prisoners, of whom eight were generals and 300 were officers. Less than half the Prussian force came into action and its losses did not exceed 500 men.[12]

LEUTHEN, ZORNDORF
AND HOCHKIRCH

Prussia had recovered but was still gravely threatened, and its subsequent victories were to be interspersed with some crushing defeats.

The only Prussian general of outstanding distinction, besides Frederick, was Ferdinand of Brunswick and he was now in command of the Anglo-German force in Hanover. The Austrian Charles of Lorraine had begun to inflict a series of defeats on the Prussian generals. He had taken Breslau. The Prussian general Bevern had been captured by Croat irregulars and his army had fled to Glogau. The Saxon and Silesian troops in the Prussian service were deserting Frederick *en masse*. Silesia was about to fall from the Prussian grasp when, a few weeks after Rossbach, Frederick arrived back in Silesia at the head of only 14,000 weary men. The command of Bevern's remnants, about 18,000, he gave to his hussar-general Ziethen.

Frederick was determined to attack, whatever the odds, although it is doubtful whether he knew that Charles, Traun and Nadasti had 80,000 men drawn up at Leuthen. The Austrian position was, however, a weak one, being extended and with too little depth, and the Austrian command was to make too many irrevocable blunders. On 5

A trooper of 5 Hussar Regiment (also known as Totenköpfe), raised in 1741 from a cadre provided by a squadron of 1 Hussar Regiment

December Frederick attacked the Austrian left, moving on it in his tactical oblique order. Fighting was particularly bitter about the churchyard of Leuthen but, at the end of the day, the Austrians were swept from the field. Leuthen, probably the greatest of Prussian victories, cost the Austrians 3,000 dead, 7,000 wounded, 21,000 prisoners and 116 guns lost. The total Prussian casualties were under 7,000.[13]

In the spring of 1758 Frederick moved into Moravia but lost his heavily escorted wagon-train of 4,000 loaded supply wagons to Austrian partisans. He then withdrew once more to Silesia.

By that summer the Russians had taken up the offensive again and, under a new commander-in-chief, Fermor, said to be of English origin (Farmer), had taken Königsberg, Thorn and Elbing before laying siege to Küstrin. Frederick marched into Brandenburg and gave battle at Zorndorf. The engagement lasted two days (26 and 27 August) and the Russians were decisively defeated in one of the bloodiest battles of the war, the Prussian loss being nearly 12,000 men and the Russian double that number.[14] Frederick was allowed no time to follow up his victory over the Russians for the indomitable Austrians were already back in Saxony and Silesia.

An officer of 2 Leib-Husaren-Regiment, formed in 1733 from the Berlin Hussars, the King's personal escort. They were usually mounted on greys

Lieutenant-Colonel von Watzmer, serving in 4 Cuirassier Regiment, was ordered in 1740 to raise a uhlan regiment of which he became chief. In 1742 this was converted to 4 Hussar Regiment

Frederick moved first into Silesia, meeting with Daun at Hochkirch near Bautzen. Frederick had encamped his 30,000 men in an untenable position facing Daun's 60,000, and he met the protests of his own Prussian generals 'that in such a situation Daun ought to be hung if he did not attack', with the arrogant retort 'that the Austrians fear us more than the gallows'. Daun did attack, however, before daylight and, although he lost 6,000 Austrians, he destroyed a quarter of Frederick's force.[15] This was the third of Daun's victories over the king in sixteen months, but the Austrian neglect to pursue permitted Frederick to keep his forces intact.

KUNERSDORF, LIEGNITZ AND TORGAU

By early 1759 the Prussian field army had been reduced to 100,000 men, many of them recruits. In August of that year a large Russian force under yet another new commander-in-chief Saltykov, was already in Frankfurt-on-Oder. There Saltykov was joined by an Austrian force under the Scot, Loudon, who had previously spent twelve years in the Army of the Tsar.

Once more Frederick hastened to attack and, during the morning of 12 August 1759, everything yielded to the impetuosity and dash of the Prussians. Half the Russian guns were taken and the king sent a courier off to Berlin announcing a complete victory. The Russians, however, were still unbroken and had dug themselves in in the Jewish burial-ground at Kunersdorf above Frankfurt. After six hours of fighting the battle recommenced, but the Prussian infantry were this time driven back with fearful slaughter. The final blow was struck by Loudon's Austrian horse which scattered the shaken, already wavering, ranks. The king was saved from capture by a handful of his own hussars as he fled for his life. Of the 50,000 men who had marched into the battle under the black eagles that morning, hardly a few thousand remained as formed bodies of troops.[16]

Frederick was fighting against impossible odds which no statesman and few soldiers would readily have accepted; he survived yet again because of the inactivity and mutual suspicions of his enemies. The Russians had refused to pursue the defeated Prussians since they believed that the Grand Duke Peter, an admirer of Frederick the Great, was about to ascend the Russian throne. So while Saltykov spent his time in debauchery, his Russian troops visited terrible ravages and atrocities on the German inhabitants of East Prussia and Brandenburg. Frederick returned to Saxony, his main recruiting ground. His arrival there was the signal for Daun to withdraw. The sneering monarch sent Finck and 15,000 Prussians to pursue; Frederick lost every single man when Daun turned on Finck, encircling his army and forcing it to lay down its arms at Maxen on 21 November 1759. A few months later Fouqué's Prussian force of 10,000 men was destroyed near Landshut by Loudon.

When this news reached Frederick he set out once more for Silesia, with the Austrians, Daun and Lacy, hanging on his flanks. He arrived at Liegnitz with 30,000 men, but since Daun had been joined by Loudon the Prussians were outnumbered by nearly three to one, while across the Oder a large Russian force stood awaiting the outcome of Daun's battle. Hearing from an Austrian deserter that the enemy intended to make a night approach to attack the Prussians before first light, the Prussians moved on the night of 14 August towards the enemy and put themselves astride the approach route. A fierce night engagement followed in which Loudon's right wing lost nearly 10,000 men.[17] Daun on the left and the Russians across the Oder declined to attack. Yet their numbers were so formidable that Frederick dared not remain on the field of battle and, at nine o'clock the next morning, he was already away, having cleared the field of guns, muskets and wounded, both Prussian and Austrian.

At the beginning of October a Russian raiding force of 20,000 had failed to take Berlin. A week later 15,000 Austrian troops under Lacy joined them and the capital was occupied for a few days, the inhabitants paying a ransom of four million thalers.

In Saxony was fought the last great battle of the war, where Frederick had returned once more for recruits and treasure. There Daun followed, to be joined by Lacy. Daun, the master of defence, had entrenched himself near the Elbe at Torgau with

A gun team of horse artillery

50,000 troops; Frederick with 44,000, was determined to attack him. Making over a third of his force to Ziethen, who had, however, no experience of higher field command, he ordered him to attack frontally on the Austrian right flank. Frederick, with the main body, made a long circuitous march of fourteen miles through the forest and attacked Daun from the rear.

Daun had 400 guns, a half of them new, and these, quickly redeploying, did fearful execution among Frederick's attacking infantry. The battle had started at about midday and was of the fiercest, but because of some confusion Ziethen's frontal attack did not materialize; by early evening the Austrians had the best of it so that the wounded Daun sent a messenger off to Vienna announcing a victory. This was Frederick's view, too, for he had withdrawn for the night, some miles away, intending to renew the attack the next day. At six in the evening in pitch darkness Ziethen's force, over five hours late, came into serious action for the first time at the place appointed for its attack to the Austrian front. Hülsen, in command of Frederick's bivouacked forces, called them to arms again and went in to attack the rear. In a few hours the battle was lost to Daun. Torgau was his last great battle, as it was Frederick's. Frederick was later to say it was the severest and most crucial battle of the war. The Prussians lost 14,000 men against an Austrian loss of 20,000 and 45 guns. Daun's army remained, however, still in being, and still ready for battle.[18]

Bosnian lancers in winter and summer uniform. On the right an officer and dismounted trooper

Finale

The strain of the war was telling not only against Prussia, which with a population of under five million was keeping an army in the field which rarely fell in strength below 100,000, but also against the French and Austro-Russian coalition, which with a population of a hundred million had nearly a quarter of a million troops in Western and Central Europe. Kaunitz warned Maria Theresa in December 1760 that Austria had resources left for only one more campaign; in the following spring the Austrian forces were reduced by 20,000 men.

Britain's new monarch, George III, wanted an end to the war and this was a widely shared feeling in Britain and France; overseas, Britain had done well and France badly and by 1762 the British subsidy to Prussia was no longer paid. In January 1762, however, the European situation was entirely changed by the death of the Tsarina Elisabeth. Her successor, the Grand Duke Peter, was a German whose principal interest appeared to be

A trooper of 4 Cuirassier Regiment, formed in 1733, but owing its existence to two companies of Hofstaats-Dragoner formed in 1671

centred in the Duchy of Oldenburg and in a dynastic claim against Denmark for Schleswig-Holstein. Moreover Peter admired Frederick the Great and mistrusted Austria. So he withdrew from the war and concluded an alliance with Prussia directed at both Austria and Denmark. Sweden also made peace. The murder of Peter some months later did not alter the political situation in that the new monarch in St. Petersburg, Catherine the Great, while having no intention of intervening on Frederick's behalf, merely confirmed the peace made by her predecessor. She ordered all Russian troops from Germany.

Maria Theresa was now isolated and in July and October 1762 Frederick won two further victories when he began to clear Silesia of Austrian troops. Realizing that she could no longer hope unaided to win and keep Silesia she came to terms with Frederick. Frederick refused to accept the mediation of Britain and France, stating his own terms of 'not a foot of land and no compensation to Saxony, not a village, not a penny'. He agreed to evacuate Saxony but held Silesia. The Treaty of Hubertusburg of February 1763 between Prussia and Austria made no alterations to the frontiers of Europe; and so 'a million men had perished but not a hamlet had changed its ruler'.

A trooper of the Regiment of Gens d'armes, the monarch's personal bodyguard originally raised in 1691. It was also known as 10 Cuirassier Regiment

1 The following Prussian regiments were present at Mollwitz: the grenadier battalions Winterfeldt, Kleist, Reibnitz, Buddenbrock, Puttkamer and Saldern; Infantry Regiments 1, 7, 10, 12, 13, 15, 19, 20, 23, 24, 25 (with a loss of 247 men), 26 (with a loss of 700 men), 27, 29; Cuirassier Regiments 5, 10 and 11; Dragoon Regiments 1, 3 and 4; Hussar Regiment 2. Casualties among general officers were: killed, von der Schulenburg; wounded, von Schwerin, von Marwitz and von Kleist.

2 The Prussian order of battle at Chotusitz (which lasted only three hours) was as follows: the grenadiers of Regiments 5, 8, 12, 15 and 16; Infantry Regiments 2, 4, 7, 10, 11, 13, 14, 15, 16, 17, 19, 24, 27 (only 400 survivors), 29, 30 and 34; Cuirassier Regiments 1, 2, 4, 5, 7, 8, 9 and 12; Dragoon Regiments 3, 5 and 7 (lost 500 men); Hussar Regiment 1. Casualties among general officers: killed, von Werdeck and von Wedell; wounded, von Rothenburg and von Waldow. Total Prussian casualties 146 officers and 4,600 men.

3 The following Prussian troops were engaged at Hohenfriedberg: grenadier battalions von Kleist, Luck, Hacke, Blankensee, Lepel, Geist, Jeetze, Wedel, Buddenbrock, Sydow, Grumbkow, Schöning, Kahlbutz, Lange, Trenck and Hertzberg; Infantry Regiments 1, 2, 3, 4, 5, 6, 7, 8, 11, 12 (took seven guns), 13, 14, 15, 17, 18, 19, 20, 21, 22, 23, 24, 25, 28, 29, 30, 31, 37 and 38; Cuirassier Regiments 1, 2 (destroyed two Saxon regiments), 4, 5, 7 (destroyed the Saxon Regiment Schönberg), 8, 9, 10, 11, 12 and 13; Dragoon Regiments 1, 2, 3, 4, 5, 6, 11 and 12; Hussar Regiments 1, 2, 4, 5, 6 and 8.

4 The following Prussian troops were engaged at Sohr (Soor or Tratenau): grenadier battalions von Wedell, Treskow, Fink, Grumbkow, Schöning, Geist, Schöning, Trenck, Kleist, Lindstädt, Stange, Tauentzien, Hertzberg, Luck, Laubenau, Finkenstein and Lepel; Infantry Regiments 2, 3, 4, 6, 14, 15, 17, 19, 23, 25 (with a loss of 244 men); Cuirassier Regiments 1 (with great distinction), 2, 4, 8, 9 (claimed to have taken three regiments prisoner), 10 (took part in Buddenbrock's attack), 12 and 13; Dragoon Regiments 3 and 12; Hussar Regiment 4. Not engaged were Infantry Regiments 11, 12, 24, 29, 30 and 38; Dragoon Regiments 5 and 10; Cuirassier Regiment 5; Hussar Regiments 1, 2 and 5.

5 At Hennersdorf Generals von Ziethen and von Winterfeldt were in command. The troops engaged were the grenadiers of Infantry Regiment 19 and the whole of Infantry Regiment 24; Cuirassier Regiments 8 and 9; Hussar Regiments 2 and 5.

6 At Kesselsdorf the following Prussian regiments were engaged: the grenadier battalions von Kleist, Schöning, Plotho and Münchow; Infantry Regiments 3, 5, 9, 10, 12, 13, 18, 20, 21, 22, 27 (with a loss of 529 men), 30 (with great distinction, all field officers being awarded the order *pour le merite*), 34, 46 (lost 600 men) and 47; Cuirassier Regiments 1, 3, 5, 6, 7, 8, 11 and 12; Dragoon Regiments 4, 5, 6, 7, 8, 9 and 10; Hussar Regiments 6 and 7.

7 Frederick reinforced the fighting strength of infantry regiments so that they stood at: 50 officers, 160 non-commissioned officers, 38 drummers, 4 pipes, 14 carpenters, 6 oboists, 12 doctors and medical attendants, 218 grenadiers, 1,220 musketeers and 7 officials (Unterstab). An independent grenadier battalion totalled 17 officers and 609 rank and file.

8 At about the time of Mollwitz the Prussian Battery Artillery consisted of twenty three-pounders, four twelve-pounders, four fifty-pounder mortars and four howitzers.

9 At Prague the following Prussian regiments were engaged: the grenadier battalions of Regiments 6, 7, 10, 22, 28, 45, 47 and 48; Infantry Regiments 1, 3, 7, 8, 9, 12, 13, 17, 18, 19, 23 (with a loss of 600 men), 24 (losing Schwerin and 450 men), 26, 27, 28, 29, 30, 31, 32, 33, 35, 37, 38, 39, 40, 41, 42, 43 and 46; Cuirassier Regiments 1, 3, 4, 5, 6, 7, 8, 9, 11, 12 and 13; Dragoon Regiments 1, 2, 3, 4, 11 and 12; Hussar Regiments 1, 2, 3, 4, 6 (took the Austrian treasure chest and 1,200 prisoners) and 8.

10 The following Prussian troops were at Kolin: the grenadiers of Regiments 9, 10, 13, 25, 31, 33, 37, 39, 42, 44 and 47; Infantry Regiments 3, 7, 1 Battalion of 15 (Guard), 17, 20 (lost 800 men), 21, 22, 25, 28, 29, 35, 36 (only ninety-seven survivors), 40 and 41; Cuirassier Regiments 1, 2, 3, 4, 6, 7, 8, 11, 12 and 13; Dragoon Regiments 1, 2, 3, 4, 11 and 12; Hussar Regiments 1, 2, 3, 4, 6 and 8; general officers wounded were von Treskow, Ziethen, Hülsen, Mannstein, Manteuffel and Ingersleben.

11 Von Lehwald's Prussian order of battle included: the grenadier battalions von Gohr, Lossow, Polenz and Mannstein; Infantry Regiments 2, 4, 11, 14 and 16; Dragoon Regiments 6, 7, 8, 9 and 10; Hussar Regiments 5 and 7 and a Bosnian squadron of 9.

12 At Rossbach the following Prussian regiments came to battle: the grenadier battalions of Regiments 7, 17, 20, 22, 25, 30 and 46; Infantry Regiments 1, 5, 6, 9, 13, 15, 19, 21, 23, 24 and 26; Cuirassier Regiments 3, 7, 8, 10 and 13; Dragoon Regiments 3 and 4; Hussar Regiment 1.

13 The following Prussian regiments were engaged at Leuthen: the grenadier battalions of Regiments 3, 12, 15, 21, 22, 24, 29, 31, 37, 40, 44, 45, 47 and 48; Infantry Regiments 1, 5, 6, 8, 10, 13, 15, 17, 18, 19, 20, 23, 25, 26 (twenty-seven officers received the *pour le merite*), 27, 30, 34, 35, 36, 37, 39, 41 and 46; the

(Left) a conductor and officer of the engineer corps and, (right) an officer of foot artillery

Freibataillone Le Noble, Angenelli and Kalben; Cuirassier Regiments 1, 2, 5, 6, 7, 8, 9, 10, 11 and 12; Dragoon Regiments 1, 2, 4, 5, 11 and 12; Hussar Regiments 1, 2, 3, 4, 6 and 8.

14 At Zorndorf the following Prussian regiments were engaged: the grenadier battalions of Regiments 1, 8, 17, 38 and 43; Infantry Regiments 2, 4, 7, 11, 14, 16, 18, 22, 23, 25, 27, 37, 40, 41, 46 and 49; Cuirassier Regiments 2, 5, 8, 10, 11 and 13; Dragoon Regiments 1, 4, 6, 7 and 8; Hussar Regiments 2, 5 and 7.

15 The Prussians engaged at Hochkirch were as follows: grenadier battalions of Regiments 3, 12, 15, 21, 27, 37, 39, 40, 41, 44, 45 and 48; Infantry Regiments 1, 5, 6, 8, 10, 11, 13, 14 (lost 1,000 men), 15, 17, 18 (almost destroyed), 19, 20 (lost 500 men), 23, 26, 29 and 30; Freibataillone von Angenelli and du Berger; Cuirassier Regiments 1, 4, 6, 8, 9, 10, 11, 12 and 13; Dragoon Regiments 1, 2, 4, 5 and 12; Hussar Regiments 2, 4, 6 and 8. Among the Prussian dead were Field-Marshal Keith, Prince Franz of Brunswick, Prince Moritz von Anhalt-Dessau and Generals von Krockow and von Hagen (Geist).

16 At the battle of Kunersdorf the following Prussian regiments were deployed: the grenadier battalions of Regiments 5, 8, 11, 13, 20, 22, 25, 26, 30, 32 and 40; Infantry Regiments 2, 7, 9, 12, 14, 16, 19, 21 (lost 700 men), 24, 29, 31 (lost 430 men), 35, 37, 39, 41, 43 (lost

550 men), 46, 47 (two officers and 600 men survived), 49 and Garrison Regiment 2; Cuirassier Regiments 1, 2, 3, 5, 7 and 12; Dragoon Regiments 2, 3, 6, 8 and 11; Hussar Regiments 1, 2, 3, 4, 5, 7 and 8. According to one account the Russian casualties were 16,000; those of the Prussians 534 officers and 17,900 men and 172 guns; twelve general officers were wounded and one (von Puttkamer) killed.

17 The following Prussian troops took part in the night engagement at Leignitz against Loudon: the grenadier battalions of Regiments 8, 12, 15, 20, 29, 33, 39 and 42; Infantry Regiments 1, 3, 5, 6, 10, 13, 15, 18, 23, 24, 26, 31, 34, 40 and 41; Cuirassier Regiments 2, 3, 5, 8, 10, 11 and 13; Dragoon Regiments 1, 2, 4, 9 and 10; Hussar Regiments 2 and 3.

18 Frederick computed the Austrian loss at about 16,000–20,000 men, but the Prussian casualties could not have been much less. Of the 6,000 Prussian grenadiers who went into battle only 600 escaped death or serious wounding; two Prussian generals, ninety officers and 4,000 men went into Austrian captivity. The Prussian regiments engaged were: the grenadier battalions of Regiments 1, 2, 3, 9, 10, 11, 14, 15, 29, 33, 38, 42, 43 and 46; Infantry Regiments 1, 5, 6, 7, 8, 13, 15, 16, 17, 18, 19, 20, 21, 22, 23, 24, 25, 26, 30, 31, 35, 41, 45 and 49; Cuirassier Regiments 1, 2, 3, 4, 5, 8, 10, 11, 12 and 13; Dragoon Regiments 1, 2, 4, 5, 6, 7, 11 and 12; Hussar Regiments 1, 2, 3, 4 and 6.

Gentlemen cadets of the Cadetten-Corps and an old soldier of the Invaliden-Corps

The Plates

A1 Horse Grenadier, von der Schulenburg's Regiment, summer field service uniform, 1729–41

This regiment was raised in 1705 by Major-General von Derffling (the son of the Great Elector's cavalry general) as 3 Dragoon Regiment and in 1713 it received the honorary title of 'Horse Grenadier' and took the grenadier type headdress into use. From 1724 onwards the regiment was commanded by von der Schulenburg, who became a major-general in 1728 and a lieutenant-general and Knight of the Black Eagle in 1740. In the early part of the First Silesian War the regiment was unfortunate. It was routed by Austrian horse at Baumgarten when acting as the king's personal escort, Frederick narrowly escaping capture; for this it lost its distinctive title and dress and reverted to dragoons. At Mollwitz it was again broken by Austrian cavalry, bringing from Frederick the retort, 'I always said those Schulenburg dragoons were no use.' Von der Schulenburg himself received a sabre cut across the face but rode back into battle where a bullet finally brought him down. Thereafter 3 Dragoon Regiment served with distinction under successive colonels, Graf von Rothenburg, Freiherr von Schönaich and Graf von Truchsess.

A2 Grenadier, Grenadier Guard Battalion No. 6, summer field service uniform, c. 1745

6 Infantry Regiment, raised in 1675 in Brandenburg, was known from 1701 as the Crown Prince's Regiment. In 1711 Frederick William (Frederick the Great's father) became its colonel and, on his accession in 1713, he raised the status of the regiment to that of the guard. Its three battalions had a total of eighteen companies, three colonels and two lieutenant-colonels, and the king recruited into this regiment, which was also known as the Potsdam Guards, all the giants he could recruit throughout Europe. For James Kirkland, an Irishman six foot eleven inches tall, Frederick William paid £1,266 sterling. In 1740 Frederick the Great allowed any who wished to take their discharge and reduced the regiment to a grenadier guard battalion. Non-commissioned officers wore the same uniform as grenadiers except for some differences in the facings; they carried a pike instead of a musket. The pike was also carried by company officers who wore a tricorne and a frock coat with silver facings and a silver waist sash.

A3 Grenadier, von Arnim Regiment (5 Infantry Regiment), summer field service uniform, c. 1729

This regiment was raised in 1672 by Colonel von Schöning and eventually became a guard or Leib-regiment. It lost this title in 1713, thereafter being known by the name of its colonel, von Arnim (later a lieutenant-general). During the Silesian Wars the regiment was commanded by von Wedell, von Bonin and, in 1755, by Ferdinand, Duke of Brunswick; the later remained as titular head until 1766, when he was obliged to give up the colonelcy on being promoted field-marshal. There was little to distinguish the uniform of the grenadier from that of the musketeer except for his headdress and the combustion case for the used for igniting grenades, was not common to all grenadiers, however, for later, when grenadiers

A non-commissioned officer of 8 Garrison Regiment, a field post rider and an oboe player of foot artillery.

were formed into battalions and regiments, they were used as élite infantry and not as grenade-throwers.

B Trooper, von Ruesch's Death's-Head Hussars (5 Hussar Regiment), summer field service uniform, c. 1744

This regiment of five squadrons was raised in 1741 in Brandenburg from a cadre squadron of 1 Hussar Regiment (originally Prussian Hussars). In 1745 it included in its strength a Bosnian sub-unit which was eventually detached and formed into an independent regiment (9 Hussar Regiment). 5 Hussar Regiment was eventually to become the most distinguished and the oldest hussar regiment in the Imperial German Army for it survived the 1806 débâcle and was reformed as two regiments of Death's-Head Hussars (1 and 2 Hussar Regiments). Its first colonel von Mackerodt died on service in Silesia and its second, von Ruesch, was Hungarian born having entered the Prussian through the Austrian service. He became a major-general in 1750 and three years later was raised by the king to the nobility (*Freiherrnstand*).

C1 Lieutenant, von Dewitz's Hussars (1 Hussar Regiment), parade and summer field service uniform, c. 1748

1 Hussar Regiment was formed in 1737 from von Brunikowski's six squadrons of Prussian Hussars, von Brunikowski being its first colonel. The regiment had to reinforce 2 Hussar Regiment (the Leib-Husaren or Berlin Hussars) and it found the squadrons which formed both 3 and 5 Hussar Regiments. The regiment gave up so many cadres and reinforcements that by 1740 von Brunikowski had only ten men left in each squadron on which to reform his new 1 Hussar Regiment. A year later, however, the regiment was already five squadrons strong and in 1724 a further five squadrons were recruited in Silesia. Its second colonel, von Dewitz, had been in the Austrian service until 1735 and its third, von Szekely, was Hungarian born, entering the Prussian through the Saxon service. Not all Prussian hussars wore the traditional and ornate Hungarian pattern tunic and dolman (*Pelz*) shown in this plate; some,

A lancer from the Bosnian uhlan squadron of 9 Hussar Regiment in close combat with an Austrian fusilier

like 2 Hussar Regiment, wore a much simpler tunic-blouse and mantle.

C2 Musketeer, von Forcade's Regiment (23 Infantry Regiment), summer field service uniform, c. 1756

This regiment was famous in that, except for the Hochkirch night engagement, it was never defeated or involved in an unsuccessful battle. It was formed in 1713 out of cadres from 1 and 13 Regiments, being raised by von Kameke. Its second colonel, in 1716, was a von Forcade, and its sixth colonel (from 1748–56) was also a von Forcade, being the son of the second. When von Forcade was appointed to his father's regiment he was already a captain on transfer from 1 White Fusilier Guard. By 1743 he was a colonel but he did not receive command of the regiment until 1747 when he had already been appointed a major-general. He and the regiment saw action at Mollwitz, Hohenfriedberg, Soor, Prague, Rossbach, Leuthen, Zorndorf, Torgau and Freiberg. At Soor von Forcade had been so severely wounded that he had been left for dead on the battlefield.

C3 Bombardier, Prussian Artillery, field service uniform, c. 1750

The artillery Bombardiere originally manned howitzers, mortars and rockets, whereas the Kanoniere found the crew for the guns. Eventually the Bombardiere became the Ober-Gefreiter. The uniform for both was similar except that the Bombardier wore the fusilier type headdress while the Kanonier had a lace-trimmed black tricorne. The number one of gun crew detachments carried a metal powder flask and sometimes a slow-match. Artillerymen were armed with only the short sword and relied for close protection on infantry or the musket-armed Handlanger, the artillery labour force which moved the guns, dug the emplacements, and brought up ammunition. Kanoniere outnumbered Bombardiere by about nine to one.

D1 Freijäger, De le Noble'sches Freicorps, summer field service uniform, 1756–63

Franz de le Noble entered the Prussian service in 1756 raising a Freicorps battalion in Naumburg, the battalion taking part in the siege of Breslau and Schweidnitz. In 1760 Noble was made prisoner but on his release three years later he was given back his old command together with two other Freicorps battalions (von Lüderitz and von Wunsch), the three forming 8 Garrison Regiment with Noble at its head. Freicorps regiments and even battalions were usually composite forces of all arms with their own Jäger and mounted detachments in addition to infantry. The Jäger shown in this plate wore a distinctive cap, somewhat similar to that used in the Austrian service, and was armed with a rifled carbine. The Frei-musketier had a similar uniform except that he wore a tricorne hat and the buttons on the tunic facings lacked the embroidered button-hole; the musketeer wore cloth gaiters instead of knee-boots.

D2 Bosniak Lancer, Bosnian Corps, summer dress, c. 1760

The Prussian cavalry was without lancers and it soon found itself at a disadvantage when faced by Polish uhlans in the Saxon service and by mounted Hungarian pandours. Frederick therefore attracted to his service deserters and prisoners from Hungary, mainly Bosnians, as well as Ukrainian

Cossacks from Galicia and even the remnants of the Zaporozhian Cossacks dispersed by Peter the Great nearly half a century before. The Bosnian lancers were formed in 1740 as one squadron of 5 Prussian Hussar Regiment and by 1760 had increased to ten squadrons. In 1763 they were reduced to only one squadron again, but in 1771 the Bosnians were back at ten squadrons and were formed into a separate regiment, known as Bosniaken-Corps Nr 9 or Regiment Bosniaken Nr 9. Although lancers they were classed as hussars, and their commander, Major-General von Lossow, was also the colonel of 5 Hussar Regiment. Officers wore a similar uniform to that shown in this plate except that the light coat was white fur trimmed, and bars of lace were worn across the chest of both the tunic and the coat. By 1770 this uniform had been replaced by one of hussar pattern, except that the baggy trousers (as shown in this plate) were retained.

D3 Grenadier, von Schony's Freicorps, summer uniform, c. 1761

Von Schony was a Hungarian who, as a major, entered the Prussian service from the Württemberg Army in 1761. He raised a hussar Freicorps in Silesia which had an infantry, grenadier and Jäger element in addition to the horse. It fought with distinction, mainly against the Russians. The hussar predominance was reflected in the pattern of the uniform of all von Schony's troops. The grenadier shown in this plate wears the tall grenadier headdress trimmed with fur, but it includes a bag. The corps uniform for infantry was similar to that shown in this plate, except for the tricorne hat. The mounted hussar wore the tunic without the topcoat, knee-boots and off-white breeches with the near conical tall headdress worn by trumpeters in the hussar line cavalry.

E Trooper, von Vippach's Hussars (4 Hussar Regiment), summer field service order, c. 1752

The Great Elector had once tried to raise lancer regiments by forming (tovarishchi) Uhlan Regiments. These Polish nationals had, however, been reclaimed by Poland. In 1740 Frederick the Great commissioned a Prussian hussar officer, Colonel von Natzmer, to recruit a lancer regiment from Poles and Lithuanians, since it was believed in those days that all good lancers came from Poland just as all good hussars came from Hungary. When, within the year, von Natzmer returned with 1,000 well accoutred lancers, Frederick was much impressed by their bearing and turn-out, so he allotted them a military operation near Grotkau to see how they would fare; at the same time, however, he took the precaution of sending Ziethen's hussars (2 Hussar Regiment) to observe their conduct. It was as well he did, for although the Poles attacked with bravery and dash it was soon obvious both to Ziethen and to the Austrians that von Natzmer's men had no training or experience in the use of the lance. Many were the wounds they inflicted on each other, and many the riders who were unhorsed when the pikes ploughed into the ground. Had it not been for the presence of von Ziethen, who extricated them, the uhlans would have been badly beaten. The uhlans lost their lances and were then reformed as 4 Hussar Regiment, still under von Natzmer until his death in 1751, and then under von Vippach. Von Vippach had transferred to the Prussian service in 1740 from Saxe-Gotha, and had spent all his former service with hussars (2 and 5 Hussar Regiment).

6 Infantry Regiment was commanded by Frederick William when he was Crown Prince. On his accession in 1713 he raised it to guard status and reformed it with Potsdamer giants. After 1740 it was reduced to a grenadier guard battalion

F1 Drummer, von Below's Regiment (11 Infantry Regiment), summer field service uniform, c. 1757

11 Infantry Regiment owed its origin to the Regiment Holstein und Spaen from which it was formed in 1685. Three years later it became the parent regiment for 20 Infantry Regiment. Von Below took over command in 1749 from Prince Frederick of Holstein-Beck on the latter's death as a field-marshal, von Below himself being a major-general at the time. He gave up the regiment in 1758 on being retired as a lieutenant-general. The uniform for drummers and bandsmen was the same as that for musketeers except that bandsmen wore the distinctive shoulder pieces and sleeves.

F2 Grenadier, von Canitz Regiment (2 Infantry Regiment), summer field service order, c. 1762

This regiment was one of the oldest in the Prussian Army, having its origin in the Elector's Life Guard Regiment (1 Infantry Regiment). In 1656 this was split, giving off Feld-Regiment Nr 2, under Prince Radziwill. Its subsequent colonels were Field-Marshal von Roeder and Lieutenant-General von Schlichting, and then Lieutenant-General von Canitz. The regiment shared the

A trooper of 2 Cuirassier Regiment, originally raised in 1666, was firstly the Elector's and then the Crown Prince's Regiment. It became a cuirassier regiment in 1731

distinctive double-button-hole tunic facing (at the waist) with 5 Infantry Regiment.

F3 Dragoon, von Gschray's Freicorps, summer field service order, c. 1761

Von Gschray, born in Mannheim in 1692, served first in the Bavarian and then in the French Army, entering the Saxon service in 1756. Having been captured by Prussian hussars when on his way to Pirna, he was asked by Frederick to raise 600 light horse for Prussia; at first he was an unwilling associate. Finally, however, in 1761 he was given a patent as a major-general and raised a corps of dragoons and infantry, about 1,600 strong, from the Nordhausen area of Saxony. His infantry and dragoons had the same uniform except that infantry wore gaiters instead of cavalry boots, and carried the short curved sabre instead of the cuirassier's straight *Pallasch*.

G1 and G2 Officer and Grenadier, 1 Battalion of the Guard (No. 15), summer parade uniform, c. 1786

This regiment was to become one of the most famous of Frederick the Great's foot guards. First raised in 1689 it was commanded by Major-General Graf von Lottum until his death in 1718 as a field-marshal, and then for two years by Colonel Freiherr von Könen. It then became known as the von der Goltz Regiment, from the name of its new colonel. Eleven years later Frederick William gave the regiment to his son (recently released from fortress arrest at Küstrin), von der Goltz being transferred to the command of 5 Infantry Regiment; 15 Infantry Regiment was redesignated as the Regiment Kronprinz. The fortunes of the regiment advanced with those of Frederick. In 1732 it took its precedence at the head of all regiments commanded by colonels, the crown prince being at that time but a colonel, but in 1735, when Frederick was promoted major-general, it advanced yet further up the lists. In 1737 it welcomed Prince Ferdinand of Prussia as a Fähnrich. When Frederick first took over the von der Goltz Regiment, it wore gold and yellow facings, but since the crown prince preferred silver and white, he obtained the royal assent to change. By a court order of 1733 the uniform colours for the regiment were decreed as dark blue with red (*echt rot*) facings (in reality some-

what tinged with brown) and yellow (*paille*) waistcoat and breeches. As with most other regiments, summer and winter uniforms were the same, except that the winter waistcoat had sleeves and was lined. When Frederick ascended the throne a few years later he reduced his father's giant guard (6 Infantry Regiment) to a grenadier guard battalion and converted his own 15 Infantry Regiment into foot guards, the first battalion being known as 1 Bataillon Garde or the Leib-Garde Bataillon, and the second and third battalions simply as Regiment Garde.

G3 Officer, Garde-du-Corps, ceremonial guard dress (Galawachtanzug), c. 1786

Immediately after his accession Frederick created his own cuirassier household troops, the Regiment Garde-du-Corps, to guard the royal household and palaces. Originally not more than a squadron strong, it was commanded by Stabs-Rittmeister von Platen, transferred from 9 Dragoons. When it took to the field it shared its duties with the Regiment Gensd'armes (10 Cuirassier Regiment). Not until 1756, with the addition of two squadrons, mainly from Saxon prisoners-of-war at Pirna, was the Garde-du-Corps made into a regiment, taking precedence as 13 Cuirassier Regiment. Since the Saxon squadrons were, not unnaturally, unreliable, they were dispersed the

Infantry officers of 18 Regiment (originally the White Grenadier Guard), of 1 Battalion of the Guard and of the Grenadier Guard Battalion

next year and replaced by Prussian cavalrymen transferred from other regiments. Eventually the regiment was raised to five squadrons, each of two companies. The officer shown in this plate wears the star of the guard and the cuirassiers' straight sword, the Pallasch; a sabretache (not visible) hangs on his left side. Other ranks on palace duty wore a similar uniform, but without fringes to the cuirass-tunic and without lace on the cap; they wore dark buttoned-up leggings, and carried Pallasch and carbine.

An officer, non-commissioned officer and miner of the miner corps

H1 *Non-commissioned officer, Miner Corps, winter field service dress, c. 1792*

The pontoniers and miners were originally one corps responsible to the artillery. In 1742 Frederick reorganized and strengthened all his technical troops, still coupling the miners with the pontoniers and pioneers and forming 49 Field Engineer Regiment under Major-General von Walrave, who was also Chief of the Engineer Corps. But not before 1756 did the miners become part of the engineer department, and only in 1773 were they rid of their connection with the pontoniers; for in that year it was decreed that pontoniers were to remain an artillery responsibility. Between 1758 and 1772 the miners establishment was increased from two to four companies, under Colonel von Castilhon, who had

come to the miners as a captain in 1742 and remained with them all his service. The miners saw much action, mainly in siege warfare.

H2 *Infantry Regimental Quartermaster, winter uniform, c. 1761*

The regimental quartermaster was an official rather than a soldier, but he wore a uniform very close to that of the regiment to which he was accredited. The same pattern uniform was worn not only by the quartermaster but also by the medical officer and the auditor. Similarly officials with the cuirassiers, dragoons and hussars wore the cavalry pattern uniform of their hosts. They were collectively known as Unterstab or headquarters supplementary staff.

H3 *Supply Detail, Commissariat (Proviantknecht), winter uniform, c. 1756*

Frederick the Great took great care in organizing his magazines, transport and supply services, so that foraging and requisitioning even on Austrian territory was an organized and controlled service; the Prussian supply personnel were a uniformed and disciplined body. Commissariat officers had a similar dress to that shown in the plate, except that they wore knee-boots instead of leggings and the tricorne was silver-laced. As officials they carried a sword.

A light infantry Jäger in a skirmish

40

INDEX

Figures in **bold** refer to illustrations. Plates are shown in **bold** followed by the caption reference in brackets.